So Many Lives, Just One Soul

Nereida Rojas-Seitz

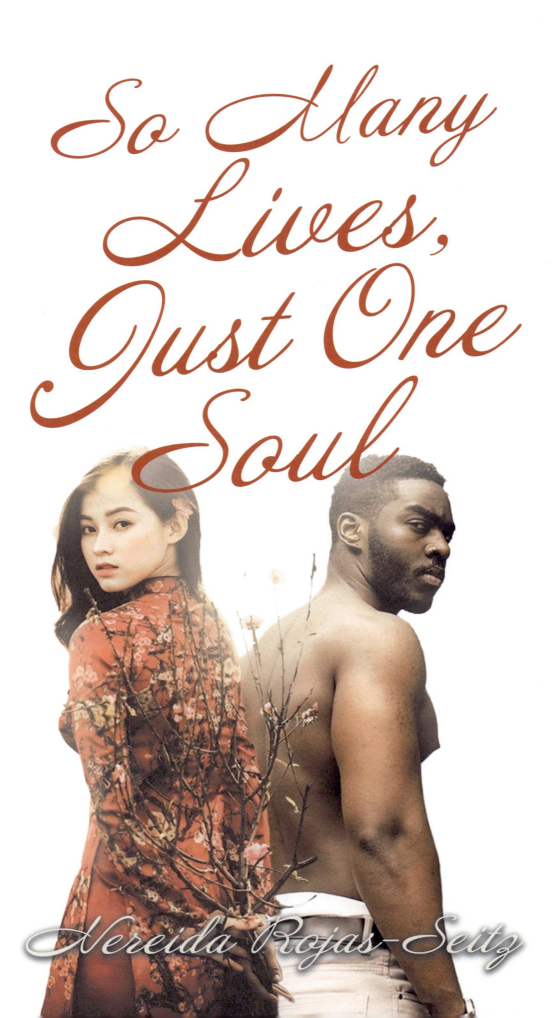

Balboa Press books may be ordered through booksellers or by contacting:

Balboa Press
A Division of Hay House
1663 Liberty Drive
Bloomington, IN 47403
www.balboapress.com
844-682-1282

ISBN: 978-1-9822-6761-2 (sc)
ISBN: 978-1-9822-6760-5 (e)

Library of Congress Control Number: 2021908275

Print information available on the last page.

Balboa Press rev. date: 11/12/2021

BALBOA.PRESS
A DIVISION OF HAY HOUSE

Contents

Introduction 1

When I first started "seeing" 3

Detoxing and Seeing Astrologically 4

Feelings 4

Soulmates and Past Lives Relationships 5

Who is Who 7

What I have learned 7

The Spirit and the Soul 8

Redo Lives 10

Research that I wanted to complete and haven't with these past lives: 10

Moving on past our Past Lives 11

Past Lives: 12

Greek Vestal Virgin 15

Speaker of the People 18

Death by my younger sister's scheming 20

Indentured Servant 21

Avi's Girl, the tutor 24

Scandinavian/Viking Woman 27

The Count of Anjou (I just love these pears, really, I do!!) 30

Native Medicine Woman 33

Angolian Captured Slave Woman 35

Daughter of a Basque Whaler 37

Wife of a Hawai'ian Chief 40

Japan 1644 43

Late 1600's, about 1688, I was born 45

Martinique 1700's 47

Prussian Soldier 51

1800's Slave in the South 54

Early 1900s Tango Dancer 59

Hawaii 1900s 62

In Retrospect 65

Introduction

Revisiting one's past lives is such an incredible experience that so many different feelings occur within the soul. There is the shock and confusion of realizing that you are not "in Kansas anymore", meaning that you are actually viewing a different lifetime, not a dream, and yet you are still involved and functioning in this lifetime. The pure awe and wonderment of which character you were, gender, race, location, the whole scene and why that particular scene at this moment of this present life, all flashes through one's mind and soul to place the puzzle pieces together.

We see, the soul feels, the mind clarifies, and if possible then luckily, history may confirm it. At least when I see the scenes, I usually can tell which character I am by the way I am feeling according to the different people who "pop" up. Then, I recognize the other people, if my soul can, by today's connections, this present life's images and relationships. Once those connections have been made, those same today's people morph into who they were in that past life.

In the beginning when I commenced "seeing" it was induced by a major pain or trauma, though now I can see at any given moment. Traumas and pains are wonderful, yes, wonderful instigators of opening up the psyche. The soul carries certain feelings within the mitochondria of the cells in different areas of the body for example, the liver carries the five R's, rage, resentment, rejection, remorse, and regret. A distinct pain or trauma can take our souls back to a previous time in which it recognizes a similar pain and/or feeling, which if we are "open" then we can see the initial fear of that pain.

How can seeing past lives help us to heal? Oh, wow, tremendously is what I say, though that doesn't answer "how". Seeing past lives helps us to heal certain fears our souls carry from lifetime through lifetime. These are fears that limit our spiritual growth, fears that encourage our ego to react in immature ways that are very illogical, no matter what age we are. We also see how we interacted with other souls that we are perhaps interacting with in this lifetime. For example, perhaps, in this lifetime you enjoy golfing with a particular person, you feel very at ease and peaceful in their presence out in nature, swinging a club. Maybe in a past life you had an experience with this same soul out in nature, or you were both part of a polo club, so in this lifetime it was practically instantaneous camaraderie between the two souls.

The soul remembers, oh boy does it remember. As of right now, I have seen over 50 lifetimes and events that were later confirmed by researching history in the part of the world. It has been fascinating and to this day I am still impressed by what our souls can do and feel. Viewing past lives is not to be taken lightly, nor without guidance, for at times one can encounter experiences that just might go against our moral ethics in this lifetime, for example, we might be a gender, race, financial caste or political affiliation that we do not care for in this lifetime. We can feel fear, relief, understanding, compassion, empathy, joy, forgiveness and acceptance, which within all these feelings help our soul heal today, leaves us lighter and allows us to spiritually connect more with the Universe and others.

When I first started "seeing"

When I first started "seeing" it was in my early twenties, I had gone to the movies with a friend of mine and ate a bunch of junk food as was typical of my age group back then, candies, soda and tons of salted fake buttery popcorn. Well, this wonderful combination exasperated IBS in my system, bloating and a bunch of burping turning into painful heartburn hiccups. Did I mention the painful hiccups? Well, the pains really scared my friend and the hiccups would not stop, so he insisted and took me to the hospital. They called my parents, so my Papi, my stepfather, came. As he awaited by my side for some prognosis of all the pain, he did Reiki on me.

This is how it all began…

I started seeing what I thought was a red flower, then the image became clearer, I saw a man kneeling, holding another man, leaning over him, in tears, while the other one died in his arms. Later on in life, the image would come back to me at different times with just a bit more detail. Finally, when I was able to afford it, I went to a hypnotist with the intention of getting more clarity, for my soul knew very well that the other person/soul that had died in my arms was someone important and I needed to know who it was and the karmic lesson behind our relationship. When I went to the hypnotist, I was very pleased that I saw another past life, just not the life with "the red flower".

I also started studying different forms of energy healing, everything from Reiki, Theta, T/EFT, Cosmic Consciousness, Huna, massage therapy, and etc. With all these teachings, I was able to see more and more tad bits of past lives, those of mine and my clients. It was so exciting!!!! Just that, not everybody wanted to know about their past lives, nor did they know what to do with that information in this lifetime, and I, at the time, could not guide them. I was just like a television for their viewing pleasure but completely ignorant on how to apply this to our present life. As I learned more about karmic lessons and relationships, the Akashic records, higher frequency, spiritual growth, astrological patterns, the doctrine of organ emotions and more, it started coming together of how this whole past lives and healing in this lifetime works.

Is my method the only one… of course not, just it has worked for me, my loved-ones and clients.

Detoxing and Seeing Astrologically

Why don't some people see their past lives and I do? I have been going through this major detox physically and spiritually. There is also an astrology lesson applied to seeing that can give it an explanation. Before this detox, I have been going through a lot of energy healings and meditations, opening up my chakras, being connected to my "inner child" and ego and allowing energy to flow.

Coincidentally, I started the cancer detox when there were eclipses conjuncting my south node, opposite my north node, which have to do with present and past lives. The combination of having opened up my pineal gland further, the eclipses and the emotional releases that the detox instigates within our cells allowed me to open up and "see" these images that caused emotional distress. With these eclipses, Pluto has been in Capricorn, and at the beginning of it all Jupiter was at the end of Libra, conjunct my natal Jupiter. I had a Cardinal Cross going on, with Pluto, Jupiter, then both Chiron and Uranus in Aries and completing this Cardinal Cross is my Ascendant in Cancer, with my Sun in Cancer. So, I had the opportunity to view these past lives.

Can others view their past lives without these astrological aspects? Of course! I am just explaining why, perhaps, I am viewing my past lives while doing the detox and others doing the detox do not necessarily "see" their past lives.

Part of writing this book is cathartic, allowing me to heal those parts of my soul that were lost and hurt. I am truly thankful for this opportunity that the Universe has gifted me and all those souls in this lifetime that have supported me.

Feelings

The feelings, opinions, belief systems and desires that I express in each lifetime comes from my soul in that particular life, not from this lifetime. So, I ask that no judgement be made, please and take it for what it is. Thank you.

Soulmates and Past Lives Relationships

Understanding the relationships, we encounter from our past lives is crucial to our spiritual growth. All this speculation about "soulmates" is genuinely vague and incomplete. What many people are looking for is a romantic partner in which they do not have to communicate verbally and hope that the other person telepathically understands the other's subdued innuendos and enjoys doing the same activities. Yup, that is what the majority of people want. It just doesn't work that way…. not in Spiritual Growth University, hahaha. Our relationships exist to help us grow and hopefully through as much fun and positive moments as possible. The more positivity that exists in the relationships, the more we want to partake in it.

The dynamics of our relationships, either in this lifetime, past lives or future lives, gives us opportunities to grow in different ways to truly complete ourselves. No one completes no one, we complete ourselves, through each lifetime. This is why we come back as different genders, races, religions, animals, political affiliations and sexual orientations to experience it all, to understand and be compassionate to all perspectives.

Certain relationships will always be parent and child, one soul older than the other, same or opposite sexes…for example, my son Wolfgang and I have several times been together as parent and child, I as the mother and he as my son, never as the same sex in that dynamic of the relationship, yet we have also been tight buddies, same sex, never have been friends as opposite sexes. My stepfather and I have always been father and daughter, he was always the father and I was always the daughter (I have no idea his proposed karmic lesson and/or tie he chose for that to happen, hahaha, I think that I got the better deal, hahaha). In these incidents, the opportunity allows the souls to guide one another, either be it from their karmic oaths they have made to one another in one way or another that it is written in the Akashic records, hence the stars, or out of pure preference and/or availability at the time in which we choose to return to another life.

As a woman in this lifetime, I have encountered several past life husbands in which I had beautiful relationships with that were deep and fulfilling. In this lifetime, I recognize these souls, especially if they are again males in this lifetime, though we feel a deep connection, we know that in this lifetime we are in each other's lives to support one another, not to be in a romantic relationship. It is those thunderbolts that we have to be weary of, oh goodness gracious… okay, let me just say that the Universe gives us these thunderbolts as a "heads up", a warning…a warning and an opportunity simultaneously.

Okay, thunderbolt relationships, if one has the stupid need to get their heart and soul a good ass-kicking through karmic lessons and finally fulfill, complete and then grow through them, then have at it. It is not easy. (I have my share of love and family karmic relationships, so I know what I am talking about, hahaha.) There is a lot of ego involved, doubting of your self-worth, heated moments (in and out of the bedroom), and finally a culmination in which either you hate one another or you both realize that you are so over "it"… then, many years later after the hatred has subsided, the acknowledgement of responsibility of one's doings in the chemical exchange of the relationship, compassion for the other person, coming to one's own acceptance of who they are…and if you really have grown sending the other person "healing loving light and best wishes" for their soul. This is why they say in astrology that it isn't the two people but the energies that the two souls create, once together.

A true and easy way to avoid the situation is when you feel that thunderbolt, tell that person, straight out… (this is where you highlight and star this paragraph and then rabbit ear the page, hahaha)" if I have ever hurt, harmed and/or disrespected you in this or any lifetime, I apologize and acknowledge how special your soul is and deserving of respect. I wish you healing loving light, much bliss, joy and peace. Thank you for this opportunity."

The most we can anticipate in any relationship is acceptance and compassion during our most vulnerable times and not to be kicked while we are down. All relationships grow because the people and their souls grow. Our needs, as humans and souls, change throughout our lives. As soon we surpass one karmic lesson, after a time of reprise, another one is in play. Our belief systems, perspectives, desires, philosophies, societal and family learnings will always be challenged by others, not because ours are "bad" but more so through those challenges we adjust our way of thinking and so do they, because though many philosophies stand true through the test of time, some are only valid during certain stages of human development as an individual and as a society.

Our growth through our relationships and at times, lack of relationships, have patterns. Astrology explains this very well, and it was well known throughout the ancient times. There is the 27-30 year Saturn Return, the 18- 22-year pattern of Saros Eclipses, the 8 year Venus pattern, certain conjunctions, oppositions, squares and trines of luminaries that we ALL encounter. So my best advice about trying to avoid certain growth pains is rush to it, embrace it, grow and heal… because quitting before the dance is done will only make you, your soul goes through it again in one of your future lives.

Who is Who

In these stories, we encounter many characters in which many I know in this present lifetime. I purposefully do not mention the connection of these past lives' characters with today's for several reasons. Some of today's people do not believe in reincarnation. Second, some of the people do not even know that they have a past life connection with me, and perhaps would not appreciate the mentioning of it. And thirdly, some of the people might have an issue with the way we were connected and/or the karmic debt that I had with that person.

I ask that this part of my past lives remains private to me and to those people involved if they choose to. A person's karmic debt is very personal, that they may not even be aware of why s/he her/himself has created it. It is disarming when a total stranger approaches you with a very personal question that everyone seems to know about and you haven't even tapped into the topic. So again, I ask that I am not questioned about who is who in today's life and if you are someone in my present life and are curious, you may ask.

If you choose to approach me about your involvement in my past lives, be cognizant that everyone does good and everyone does bad (at least in other people's perspectives), so finding out about your past life can be an eye- awakening experience for you.

What I have learned

"Seeing" all my past lives have taught me so much. I am still amazed at the details of history that we are not taught in school. Is there even time to learn all the details of actual history? And how can we choose what is important to learn? What is important for one soul is probably frivolous to another. So aside from factual history taught in school, I had to research after "seeing", because my scientific mind sometimes still doubts what I "see", hahaha.

I am always impressed at the little confirmations such as, the Portuguese in Africa as early as the early 1500's and they arriving in Brazil in 1500. Wow!!! I never knew that. I learned that the Romans were in Northern Scotland, Caledonia in the new millennium of JC. I learned that in Martinique, there were both Black and Creole slave owners, meaning the slave owners were African descendants. I learned about early Canadian colonies, and their Basque whalers. The integration of the Filipinos and Japanese in Hawaii in the early 1900s was very educational for me as a present day Hawai'ian Hula coach and answered why there were Hawai'ian songs with Portuguese lyrics. The adrenaline junkie Captain Matthew Webb explains my adventure seeking ways. The Greek Vesta Virgins (which were actively sexual) gave me insight to my tantra interests. Many more lives that include the Patriotic War of 1812, the Italian/Jewish migration to Argentina in the late 1800s, female Ninjas of 1600s Japan, 1200s witch trials, the California Native Americans of the Costa Mesa area travelled often to Catalina and Ventura..of course, the locations had different names, the real first Crusades of the late 900s, the Vikings, the Calphs of 800s, and the Dorset people all have made my soul the energetic vibration it is presently and wonderfully.

Oh my gosh, I am overwhelmed with excitement of how our people, meaning human existence has existed, how emotionally and spiritually evolved we were, and how historians make it seem that the losers had childlike minds and the victors were the only civilized. It also saddens me that many humans gave in, believed in condemning another group for their own prosperity and abundance, stripping both themselves and their victims of any human and spiritual dignity, and that they encouraged the false idea of scarcity (there is always enough for everyone!)… and, sadly, it continues… and for what? The people all die, their souls end up fulfilling other karmic debts for soulfully internally reasons that only that soul knows and yet the vicious institutes that they created that condemn other groups of people still exist… how stupid are humans!!!!!! It is not okay, to continue this way.

On the other hand, (and I thought about this as I was washing dishes…which I actually find peace in doing…and sharing my thoughts with my son, as he was pressing his celery juice) that the stupidity of some humans give the opportunity to other humans to teach society about physical and internal strengths, moral issues, and a platform to fulfill our soul purpose. If we pay attention to every century, every twenty years actually, there is some kind of struggle between a group that is being oppressed and a group trying to dominate. Hence and sadly, the cycle continues.

The Spirit and the Soul

Writing about all these past lives and recalling my soul's experiences, joys and pains have really led me to believe that there is a difference between our soul and our spirit. After I write about one past life, I do a healing on it, releasing all the pains, guilts, sorrows, the five R's, shame and despair. In the midst of the healings, I come to realize that those pains separate us from our spirit. Our soul carries all our experiences and connections to our past and present lives, the "good" and "bad", our karmic debts and purposes of serving humanity, mankind and nature.

Our spirit is our connection to the Universe, God, the Divine Creator and all the wonderful heavenly beings. While it seems that with every life time our soul separates more from our spirit, and yet the goal is to reconnect our soul with our spirit as one, eliminating all negative feelings that are imposed upon us by religions, society, family and personal thoughts and filling us with the universal unconditional healing loving white light that makes us whole.

By understanding the Universal Essential Laws, we heal the feelings of separateness and bring ourselves closer to being whole. The fight within us makes us feel undeserving to be complete because we have chosen to have a 3D experience, as if we have condemned ourselves for wanting more than a spiritual connection. It is not the denial of our 3D bodily connection that makes us whole but the moderation, balance, compassion and love for ourselves that we have within this dimensional experience that fulfills us. During this treading of time, space and dimensions it is part of our Karma to understand that we can only have high expectations of ourselves and not of anyone else and to still have compassion for others striving to reconnect their souls with their spirits.

Redo Lives

Writing about my past lives as an astrologer, I have been able to clarify certain information through reviewing certain charts. As an astrologer, I would think that when someone had a redo life, that the karma debts were from the most recent of past lives. Or if their next life is a redo life it is from the karma debt of their present life.

It doesn't work that way at all. There can be hundreds of lifetimes in between with thousands of years separating those two lives that are intertwined. An example I have that occurred with me was the life in Caledonia, late 80's AD and the life as a male African-American slave in the early 1820's AD. That is practically 1700 years apart, (and my ego says... better late than never, hahaha). This is also reassuring because we are now aware that our souls will at some time or another fulfill their karmic debt to evolve one step closer to reuniting with our spirits.

Research that I wanted to complete and haven't with these past lives:

So, before I wanted to actually write this collection of lives, I had wanted to "connect the dots" so to say. I wanted to see if there were any significant similarities, connections, astrological aspects, if the locations created a physical symbol, were the locations on ley lines, and any pattern in which I reencountered other souls, but I haven't gotten to answer all those questions. I have been very encouraged to write this ensemble by others, reminding me that I can always have a second edition, hahaha.

So, yes, all those questions that you have, I also have and hope at some time to answer them. Also, I have wanted to be hypnotized in hopes of filling in any present blanks in those past lives. I noticed that I hardly see the mundane everyday life routine of those lives, just extreme emotional events, both joyous and heart wrenching.

Moving on past our Past Lives

With tears, there is a certain pain, guilt and remorse that I feel as I move forward, having fulfilled my karma and healing my past lives. There is almost a sense that I am abandoning them. I do know that I need to move forward, and yes, I am excited to do so, and I know that it is best for them (my soul in those lives), hahaha. I am even laughing about it... from tears to laughter because I know that all projects have a beginning and an ending. So, it is time to add something new to my life. This can only happen if I create space, by leaving behind these past lives and those souls that are not in this present life. By doing this I create space for newness. This has all been a good thing. Healing these past lives and their karmic debt has been very relieving, having done wonders with my heart and soul. Even to just have to accept the incomplete karmic debts, and that that is just how it is and some of it is not even my fault. In fact, it is very egotistical to think that I had some kind of power to change their lives and their energies. We have to remember the Laws of Manifestation and that other souls have their own purpose and karmic debts and they manifest according to themselves, including the negative aspects. Being aware of that, I relieve myself of any guilt and of any karma of leaving, moving on and that I am not abandoning anyone. Also, codependency is not what we are here to do. We are here to be independent and in control of our own karma and life purpose. We have the power to choose. We can choose to do with or without the support of our loved ones and in doing so we create our future.

Past Lives:

100 BC Medicine Man in the Jungle
Years: 100 BC
Gender: Male
Location: Central-Southern Mexico, today

I remember walking through the jungle after a fresh rain, seeing the vibrant flowers and the different shades of green, being accompanied by my faithful black panther Eignyoc. The feathers of the birds almost pass for the colorful petals of the flowers. I am content, serene, at ease with who I am. The jungle is my home and I am its caretaker.

I am a healer, a magician and one with Mother Nature. I have travelled from the Caribbean to the Pacific and back again. I am well known as a healer and a magician. I do not know my biological parents. I was raised by a well-known healer of his times, who was also the village leaders' magician, a warlock, a shaman.

At one point my guardian was confronted by an evil witch in front of the village leaders. She was evil because she consulted with spirits that required live sacrifices which was not part of my guardian's beliefs nor teachings. She challenged him and in the process, from a distance, I had decided to help him, without alerting him. It was in good intentions that I was helping him out, though, later I was found out, he was ridiculed and I was ousted from the village to save my guardian. It was the first time I actually feared for my guardian's life, and to save him I agreed to flee… I missed him dearly. He taught me everything, how to get food from the ground, the trees, the bushes, to heal with nature, how to anticipate human nature, how to read the weather and the stars, how to talk with the animals but not how to deal with people.

I taught the world of natural medicine and the wonders of nature from village to village. Though I was happy to arrive, I was just as happy to be alone with my panther.

In my teens, I had conceived a baby girl that was born dead and her mother, my wife that I had dearly loved, died soon after, within days. They had tried to use snake venom to coagulate her blood. It is after this incident that I started travelling more and when I had befriended my Eignyoc.

From village to village I had acquired more and more pupils. In one village, in particular, the same town where I was raised, I had a very young and apt pupil, to only find out later, that his mother was the "evil witch". She was older now, and I competed with her to show her my worthiness to teach her son. She was apt in the wonders of the four elements though I won her respect.

As time continued, her son, one of my best pupils, became very fluid with the elements and able to command them with such ease and simplicity.

I remember "seeing" as I enter a village, the people running to me, telling me that "he" is out of control, that "he" isn't respecting the protocols of magic, that he plays with the elements "just because" and for entertainment and that it is affecting the crops and the villagers' harvests. The village leaders find it funny and do not care that the harvest is affected and still demands that their fees are paid.

This "magician" was one of my star pupils, as I "see" him, he seems intoxicated with something, some herb or liquid. He is behaving a bit pompous, not at all humble, expressing an overzealous sense of pride and godliness. I have tears in my eyes and feel slightly responsible for this behavior for having had indulged him too much and not enforcing more self-discipline and respect. He greets me whole-heartedly with much reverence and that thrills me, not so much for my ego, more knowing that he still respects me and my teachings. I must do something, I must do something. I go meditate the next day for most of the day. In doing so, I realize that I must "adjust" a certain teaching for he won't stop, so I must "disempower" him, somehow, so that way he is no longer harming the crops, hence the villagers. He is supposed to be their healer, their counselor not their enemy.

I approach him, and I tell him that he is of age and should consider sowing his seed (now this is a contradiction from what I had taught, which was that celibacy made one more in touch with the Universe. (As I write this I am shaking my head, because I now know in this lifetime that we can be both human and spiritual, that it doesn't have to be neither one nor the other.)

I encourage him to take a consort of some sort. I instruct him on the ways of love making so that way with each orgasm he loses his power. It is truly sad for me as his teacher and friend to do this and see it happen, yet, it needs to happen. He slowly loses his powers and hence loses his favoritism from the village leaders and his consort. He is practically destroyed.

I do not see what actually results, for I leave in the beginning process of him losing his power (which I find, in this lifetime, a bit cowardly and not friend like, to leave my pupil stranded), but I knew no other way to make good with the Universe. I took it as my responsibility and that it was my fault for the type of person/ magician he had become.

In this present lifetime that pupil is my son. It is my obligation to teach him discipline and spiritual growth while living a three dimensional life and still have balance and bliss. I have seen when I wasn't his parent in past lives that I encourage a certain sense of excess, debauchery and panism and witness his own undoing. So in this lifetime as his mother, I try to teach him balance and responsibility for being a human, healer and a man. Also, my karma in this lifetime is to detach my sense of worth from my son's sense of being. I have to be content with the fact that I have taught him all that I could and ultimately it is his choices that makes him who he is and that is also his karma, no longer mine. I love you Wolfgang, you are your own man. I will always have an ear to listen to you and always respect that you are you.

Greek Vestal Virgin

Year: 40 BCE
Location: Today Greece
Gender: Female

I was a Greek Vestal Virgin with my own bath spa, where people, both females and males came to detox and cleanse. I had a group of ladies and some men, all ages from 13 to 60 years of age who helped run the spa for the benefits and health of the people.

The people arrived to detox, they would spend the day and sometimes, a day and a half. This was their time to relax, regain consciousness, to expel all the negative intakes over the past month or so, to feel compassion and kindness, to treat their body and soul as the temple that they are. At the Spa, it was a time of cleansing, relaxing, rejuvenating and rehabilitation. This ceremonious ritual of the body and soul caretaking involved at least three or more of the following: a cleansing bath, fruit, herbs, oils, crystals, different styles of massages, energy cleanses, a swim, tantra, prayers, meditations, dance and vegan meals.

This was our life, healing people. Many of our patrons were well known and had an important voice in society. They came from near and far. We also tended to civilians of natural state. The treatment the patrons received depended upon the analysis, what could be afforded and what was most dyer for the patron's well-being. I usually did the analysis.

The spa would be closed every fortnight for two days for rehabilitation of my vestal virgins. This was necessary since they gave so much of themselves, it was so important that they reconnect deeply to the universe, nature and gods to rejuvenate themselves to be able to give the best to our patrons.

Some of my vestal virgins, after the age of 35, would be hired on a private level for a household on a permanent basis to tend to that family.

The building was more like a temple, high ceilings, white and black marble and blue tile. We had musicians in almost every room. There were the ceremonial baths and the detoxing baths, an area for the tantra communion, massages, meditation and eating areas. We had a garden outside that we tended to. For some patrons, our temple was a piece of heaven, an escape to rejuvenate themselves, a place to feel unconditional love and acceptance, a sanctuary to release all their pain and self-destruction, where answers were found and new plans were formed, and a forum where their voices and needs were heard and tended to with compassion.

I had a favourite particular patron. He was a general of some sort, tall, handsome (strong chin), gregarious laughter, hazel-blue eyes, and a strong built. He was the father of my two youngest children, a boy and a girl. The girl was older by almost two years, and he loved them equally, yet it was never said that they were his children. He just had a knowing. We never talked about it, he on his own volition just started to interact with them and take them as his own whenever he was in town.

I never straight out told him, for as a vestal virgin that was our knowing and our life. We were the wives of many, we shared our tantra energies to heal the souls of the land so that they may easily and flowingly fulfill their life purposes on earth. We were their earthly angels. We belonged to no one and no one belonged to us, not even our children. Our children were declarations of the gods that we must continue to tend to the earthly pained souls.

I had a total of three children. My eldest I had her when I was 15 years of age, just barely starting as a vestal virgin. Her father was a priest who taught me about tantric exchange of energy, he was no longer living. He actually used to run the temple, I took over while he was ailing and could no longer tend to the daily concerns of running the temple. My sister, and yes, a blood-sister and my eldest daughter helped me run the temple.

We had our own temple laws to secure the smooth running of the temple for example and the most important: continuous emotional detachment of the patrons with our vestal virgins. Some of the laws were as simple as the wearing of a certain colour by the virgins which stated the station for the day, such as green working in the garden, white meant tending to the patrons, yellow in the kitchen and I wore violet often.

The temple's children would run around in the gardens and were taught by my eldest daughter the basics of life, stars, math, some history and philosophy. We loved each other's children as our own. By the time the children could walk, they helped tend to all the gardens, learning about herbs, flowers, vegetables and fruits. At the age of ten the children would help out with small errands and chores of the temple. At the age of 14 they were taught in the ways of tantra and healings. If a vestal virgin left or abandoned her/his station, the children had to stay at the temple. This was more as a precautionary reason for society didn't really accept other children unless the parent had passed away. So to keep the children safe, protected and loved we kept them at the temple.

At times we were hired out to perform ceremonial tantra healings at private residence near and far. My experienced vestal virgins would arrange and perform these ceremonies. If one of my vestal virgins returned pregnant, they were never to tell the biological father for we had an oath as not to disturb the lives of our patrons just to offer positive energy and support.

Though we were a slice of heaven on earth, I had to be aware of the politics in the surrounding areas, for there was always a war going on that could affect our temple by either and/or both land and philosophical views. Though it is necessary to state that we were well protected by the patrons and government, who saw the need and importance of the vestal virgins existence.

I died at the age of 80 years, content that I had fulfilled my life purpose, serving the gods and the people, and having left a legacy for my children.

In this lifetime, I had a deep love for the father of my two youngest children and was always deeply joyed in receiving him. At the same time, I never lamented being a vestal virgin. I accepted the fact that this was the way of the world in which I lived.

Speaker of the People

Born: 40 AD/CE
Location: Caledonia, present day Scotland
Gender: Male
Wife, 6 years younger than I, three-four children

The synopsis is that I am happily married to a very good woman, whom I love dearly. The harsh bottom line is that my wife and youngest two children, the youngest was 7 years of age, were killed by the Romans. I was an important chieftain who led the Caledonians against the Romans, which we won.

I fought for our rights, for our freedom and for our land. I was very outspoken and when I had returned from battle, my wife had been hanged and the youngest two children stabbed and throats cut open. I was 43 years of age at the time of this battle. I remember coming back from war and seeing the dead bodies of my beloved wife and children, my eldest son telling me what had happened and how he found them this way when he had returned. I was angry, devastated, resentful and hating the enemy far more than I ever had.

It seems that I became ill or perhaps depressed and something happened with my right leg. I and my second son lived with my eldest son and his wife, my daughter-in-law, after the battle. My daughter-in-law kindly and generously nurtures me back to health. I remember that the soups she would make me touched the depths of my soul. I cried a lot for my loss, for my family's loss. My youngest living son was about 10 years old and deeply needed my attention, but for a few months I was lost within my loss.

I would remember how my eldest son would come to me with talk about the rights of the people to motivate me to get out of the home, but I felt dead, bitter and without energy. My daughter-in-law would have my youngest son come to me and attempt to play with me, anything to engage my spirit to be in the present. She really taught me to be in the moment, that it was better to have loved and lost than never experience it whatsoever.

As time progressed, my eldest son became a "politician", my youngest living son grew strong and I am proud of both of them. And my beautiful daughter-in-law was my living angel. Her daily smiles, positive words and delicious meals helped me heal and to remind me that I still have another two children to continue to love.

I always kept the guilt of my wife's and two children's death deep inside of me. Blaming myself for their deaths. I chose to not ever get too active again in politics and just concentrated on cultivating the land and tending to the animals.

If only I had been there to protect them, we would all be a family. I love my little family, though I dearly miss my big family.

I owe her, my wife, I owe my two sons, somehow, I shall make it up to them, and free them. I died at about 57-60 years of age.

Death by my younger sister's scheming

Time: 500's AD
Location: Taiwan, Hong Kong area
Gender: Female

So, I was married to a village leader. He had only married me so that way he could marry my younger sister. Since I wasn't married yet when the village leader approached my father about marrying my younger sister, my father made the deal that the village leader would also have to marry me since I was the oldest. Being that I was married to the village leader first meant that I had First Wife privileges, acknowledgements and responsibilities which included the finances.

I do know that my husband really loved my younger sister. My husband and I had three children together and he also had children with my younger sister. Even though I knew about his preference for my sister over me, I was quite content with life. I had beautiful children, we were provided for, had a good home and the village people were kind to us. I was unaware of my younger sister's discontent, mostly in preoccupation with her children's inheritance, for I had given birth to my husband's eldest son and daughter before my younger sister gave him children.

I "see" that there is a battle going on and I was to guide the children into hiding. As we flee, I am struck by a poisonous arrow and I faint. When I come to, I find out that two of my children have died and now I am being accused of killing them. The poison is strong and is taking control of my body. A runner was sent out to collect herbs to counteract the poisonous arrow yet it is too late. My father accused my husband for my death when in reality it was my younger sister's scheming that brought the death of my two eldest children and me.

From this lifetime I learned the lesson to not impose myself onto others and to know when to "leave". Though it was on my father's insistence and not my own, I saw how I was so unwanted and slowly looked upon with exasperation and resentment by my sister and my husband, my husband mostly to please my sister. Now, in this lifetime, I have learned to read when I am no longer wanted in a situation and knowing when to not even get involved, just keeping my limits and boundaries.

Indentured Servant

Year: 800CE
Gender: Female
Location: Today Poland, Vistulans West Slavic

****Just a heads up, there is sexual content in a submissive and dominant experience (similar to BDSM). If you are not yet on this spiritual level, please skip to my next lifetime.

Oh no, I was a bad girl, a truly bad bad girl. How could I have known, I was only a child, a young girl, a newly teenager of 13 years, who fell for the gallant charms of a prince who happened to look at me twice. He looked at me, at ME!!! He told me beautiful phrases that I never thought that I deserved to hear or would even ever hear during my lifetime. He was beautiful and I, so open, wishing it was true. How was I to know that he was just playing me, extracting information from me regarding our townspeople's planned rebellion?! I was so young, naïve, yearning to be loved and just a girl. The prince took my virginity and I blindly told him everything, who and what of the rebellion. I believed in the seduction of a prince to be true only to betray my master's family, all in the name of love, or at least what I thought was love at 13. The prince made a mockery of me and I now was stained, forever, at least this is what at 13 I believed.

I was an indentured servant/slave by my parents to the town's main ruler. They had a son about 7 years older than myself. I lived to be between 51-55 years of age.

As a servant to this prominent family I had duties that allowed me to be within hearing distance of privy conversations. The townspeople were tired and frustrated with the "governor's" laws and over taxation. They were planning a rebellion and to sell their crops on their own to neighboring counties without the governor's knowledge.

After I was used and discarded, I ran back to my master's home for I had nowhere else to turn to, where I begged for forgiveness, pleaded my case to naivety and stupidity, and indentured myself to them for the rest of my living days in return for safety and my life. My master's family was ready to rid me to the townspeople, to allow them to make an example of me and to kill me. It was their young son who saved me. He took responsibility for me. I was now his personal slave until my dying days. But first I had to make up for reparations, for the rebellion was squashed by the governor and his princely son, all because of me.

My "new" master did make an example out of me. He explained to me that I had done bad, real bad and must be punished and the townsmen must be assuaged. The male townspeople wanted revenge, so my master had me tied up, bent over some logs, blindfolded, bare, nude as the day I was born and offered me up to the townspeople for a whole day and night as long as I was not stabbed. Many had their way with me, and at times, more than one. I was spanked, slapped and even kicked.

Nothing mattered, my Master gave me life and I loved him for it. I am nothing without him. He is my everything. I do not even know or care if Master has a wife, I am alive. I am alive because of him. I do everything and anything Master commands of me, it doesn't matter because he gave me life, and I am alive.

Master has me follow strict rules of maintaining the home and serving and entertaining him and his buddies. But all that doesn't matter, I have a home, my own home that I take care of and in which Master and I make love all the time, though I am not sure what we do is making love. At least I think that it is. I serve my Master on my knees, cooking his favourite meals, serving his drinks, and I dress, if I do, the way Master commands me.

There is a lot of sexual activity which includes him sharing me often with his buddies. I do not care, I am alive and he "loves" me. Every night, I am on my knees orally relaxing him, shaking my tail, making him so happy. At first our "love" is one of him "saving" me and his resentment towards me. As I become a woman, I notice that he looks at me with a wanting. He has me wear copper wire jewelry around my nipples. I can make him laugh and at times, he likes to remind me that I am not his wife, but his slave and I am for his taking as it pleases him. I do not mind for this is all I know since I was 13 years of age and I know that he does love me in his heart.

There is a yearly celebration where they dress like wolves. I am to run out, naked and the men go on the hunt to capture me. I am devoured for their taking. (When I first saw this scene, for the longest I created a block to "see" more because I was devastated and appalled that I had sex with what I saw as dogs. It took a few meditations, forgiving of me and my master of what happened and clarity as not to create karma debt from that lifetime. I share this because sometimes seeing into our past can be harsh and a lot of compassion and understanding is needed to view these lives.) We get spirited away with the liquids, some seem like a potion. I am taken by more than one at any given time, all under the supervision of my Master. At first when this debauchery happened, I was scared, horrified and I hated myself for it. Master told me since I was so willingly giving it away to the prince it was now time to learn a lesson. Years later, I look forward to the annual ceremony and to the annual punishment that I continue to receive as a reminder of my trollop ways as a teenager. I know that Master looks forward to them also. I play that I am scared and beg for forgiveness and He plays at being angry and stern…we all play.

When the children are old enough they are sent to a training "school" of some sort. We had two boys and a girl. I receive letters from them often which He reads to me. I see them seldomly. If Master had another family, it was not of my concern. I was alive, my children provided for, I had a home and Master was with me often. I am thankful… my life is His, as it should be. I died by the hands of my Master through asphyxiation during one of our sexual interludes, and I wouldn't have wanted to die in any other way. I died orgasming into the eyes of my Master and it was bliss all the way.

In this lifetime, I am very submissive due to my deep and intense gratitude for my life. "Seeing" this life as a woman in my present life had at first caused me despair in thinking how weak and self-deprecating I was. I had to go deep within my soul to feel exactly what was going on to be open to "see" more while detaching any present day emotion to block and judge myself in that lifetime. As I "saw" more, I realized that there was no sense of shame to be needed let alone to release nor forgive, for that was life at that time for me, and my soul is very much at peace with it.

Avi's Girl, the tutor

Time: early 860's CE
Location: Egypt-Present Toledo, Spain
Gender: Female

We, my father...my Papi and I, are crossing the desert. I know that he has fear, yet I am filled with security and deep admiration for my father. He tells me that we are fleeing. I only know what my younger self is told. My mother died in childbirth. We were Jews that lived in a mostly Muslim nation.

My father was an advisor to the Caliph. Due to the constant warring and fearing that we would no longer be protected, Papi and I fled through the North of Africa. (I just want to add, that from a point of view of a child, this is one of my favourite lives. Most lives I do not recollect from birth all the way to death, just certain time spans yet this one I recall from very young until my death.) Our travels lasted more or less about three years. I grew a lot in many ways during this time.

Along the journey, my Papi taught me languages, literature (mostly poetry, for it was always wittier to tell a story in a rhyming fashion), astronomy (which included today's astrology), math and finances. I was in so much awe of what my Papi knew and in so much anticipation of the next lessons. I relished our time together. I was constantly learning from all that was mentioned, including cooking and human nature.

I can see it clearly on many nights, lying on our backs, my Papi pointing out the stars to me, their constellations and their meanings. During the times we encountered other people, my Papi taught me the details of bartering and the worth of what we had and knew. Because of his languages, he was able to get good deals with practically everyone, and many times we would join in with other caravans.

Sometimes we would encounter other nomads and travelers. We would exchange goods. I know for sure that we had spices, sometimes beans and other food items, yet vegetables and fruit were delicacies for which I would get excited. Sometimes, if my Papi was in a good mood towards me, he would exchange goods for cloth material so that way I could have new clothes.

One day, my Papi and I met a family. We camped out together for a couple of weeks. There was this lovely woman, at least I thought that she was a woman, hahaha, whom we met with her father and sisters. They were Muslims. She was kind with a beautiful smile, she sang songs that were familiar to us. She was elegant, kind, compassionate, good with cooking and finances. My Papi fell in love. I liked her very much, I think that I was in daughterly love, since I never grew up with women before except the ladies that would take care of the house back in Egypt. They were "married" and then we three continued our journey West.

She was very kind to me. She taught me the ways of womanhood. I learned even more cooking techniques besides what my dad had shown me. She was very loving with me. I was truly happy to have a woman role model, a "mother". My papi was happy also, to feel like a complete whole family. She loved him and he adored her, the energy was so beautiful, for a while life was perfect, even as we were travelling.

Our happiness was cut short within a year and a half. While my papi was gone trading with another group, some travelling robbers came. My new mother tried to protect me, they stabbed her, leaving her to die. I tried to help her with no avail. By the time my Papi returned to our campsite our lovely new family member had died. He was devastated. We were heartbroken. We took her back to her family and were involved with the end of life rituals. And then we were on our way again.

Our travelling time took about three and a half years.

While at our destination, in the Iberian Peninsula, (Toledo, Spain). Here, again my Papi was an advisor to the Caliph and I was the prince's tutor. I was only a few years older than he, but during the years he grew much taller than I and into a very becoming young man. Several times, my father suggested a different tutor for the Prince but the Prince rejected those ideas and demanded for me to continue to be his tutor.

As time progressed, the insistent Prince charmed and seduced this young pure Jewish woman. We weren't sure what we were doing intimately, though he was just so irresistible that the pull towards him was intense and led the way. Many days I would be remorseful for what we were doing since we knew that we would not get our parents' consent, then he would just kiss my guilt aside. He fascinated me and it did not happen all at once, for he was ten when I started tutoring him and I was about fourteen and now he was a dashing seventeen-year-old, strong, able body and witty mind and very worldly and knowledgeable, of course, I taught him everything he knew.

It was hard to deny the muscles in his arms and developed legs, the upper chest hair peeking through his shirts and the scrubby dirt mustache around his lips. His smile was huge and always made me happy from within. His jealousy was obvious that our fathers were starting to notice the Prince's behaviour towards me was more than of a sisterly sort.

A couple of times, my father tried to marry me off but the Prince proclaimed that he still needed me and was not yet ready to dispense of my tutoring. The Prince had a hold on me, and I was just tickled pink and proud.

All during this time, I also had learned from my father about health and remedy tinctures. I worked often and sometimes, long hours in the gardens and chamber growing and mixing herbs, flowers and seeds for the court people.

By the time that I was 22 years of age, I was pregnant with the Prince's baby. As it became more noticeable, my father sent me away, down south to live with his sister and hide the "shameful" fact that I was pregnant out of wedlock and that also that the Prince was to have a child. It was from one moment to another, I never was able to say goodbye to the Prince, for he was off in a battle.

In southern Spain, I lived with my aunt and ran an herb tea and tincture shop for the town and assisted with healings for almost six years. I never saw the Prince again and he never found out that I was pregnant. He had died in that same battle. I gave birth to a beautiful baby girl.

There were many battles due to the often uprisings of the rebels. In one of these uprisings, which happened in our town, I was killed, my throat slit in front of my six-year-old daughter and my aunt. I had rushed back to the shop to lock up everything and hide anything of precious value. As I came out, I saw my aunt holding my daughter back. I yelled for her to take her home because the rebels didn't care for us Jews, and one of them came behind me, yelled something, wrapped his arm around me and slit my throat. As I was dying, I saw the horror on my poor daughter's face and the helplessness of my aunt.

This lifetime, I had a beautiful love affair, a beautiful daughter and the upbringing of a wonderful man that I am so thankful for.

Scandinavian/Viking Woman

Year: 900's
Born: 939
Wedding: 957
Died: 1010
Gender: Female
Astrological notes: NN: Cancer Pluto: Cancer Uranus: Gemini Neptune: Leo Saturn: RetAries Chiron: Pisces Jupiter: RetSag-Sco
Location: Iceland and other Scandinavian Countries
Daughter of an important well-known trader.

I "see" myself standing tall, hair up wearing both a shell or bone comb and a metal one, wearing a combination of seal skin with a white fur. On a boat with a high front. I am a very proud woman who smiles yet not a big smile, a knowingly smile. I am elegant and strong.

I have a good husband. I see a peacock symbol by my husband. He is very handsome and tall with a gregarious laugh. My husband already had a son, out of wedlock before marrying me. A total of nine children in our household (I do not think that they are all mine, a couple are my nieces and nephews, out of protection for her, yet I am not sure why). We have homes in different locations, one in Iceland and back at the homeland. My husband, sons and nephews travel far and wide to trade. They encounter people from different areas. I have a couple of indentured servants that help me with the children. I love to travel, feeling the wind against my face. It seems that I am literate, I can read and write though at this time I cannot tell the language. I just see that I am looking at what looks like some sort of paper.

My father is a well-known warrior and trader. I have "seen" different scenes that upon arrival from a boat to a tiny port, that the village people are so excited to see us. It seems that every time we arrive and are to leave that there is a gathering of good food and mead of some sort. I write accounts from our travels.

I am the eldest of my siblings, before I married, I was involved in a battle with my father and brothers, I am good with a bow and arrow, I have killed three men.

Okay, there is a scene that concerns my present day self, it shows the bitchy, "do not give a care about anyone else and I am into revenge", ouch!!!! So, here goes… There is a scene where I had seen my nephew, the one that I raised real closely with my eldest son, talking with a young lady, she had already denied my son. I can feel my anger and jealousy, "how could she deny MY son?!" I rush home to my children and convince my sons that they have to get revenge on their cousin. I go with my eldest and two other sons. My eldest approaches the "couple" my nephew and the young lady, probably only 17 years of age, voices become loud, my sons move forward, and with a flick of a wrist my nephew stabs and kills my son. I am ashamed for my jealousy, for my son's "weakness", for having raised my nephew (of course, he was going to be prepared, I raised him) and for my stupidity that cost my son's life. I am angry with the world because I am angry with myself, I should have stayed out of "it". My eldest didn't even want to go nor approach his cousin about the ordeal, it was me who pushed him. My husband will be furious. And now, there is a feud between my sons and their cousin, and I instigated it all, unfortunately.

After the funeral ceremony, I tell my husband that I want to leave, I am going on his next trading trip. I couldn't stay to bear the pain and my inner humiliation. I want to hurt the girl, she should have been with my son. Stupid girl, what does she know. (When I write these past lives' experiences, I stay true to the feelings that are going on at the time, even if my present self doesn't agree with the choices I have made in the past.)

I need to focus on my daughters, they are getting older and prime to be wed. I am a bit cold and bitter woman, I try to show affection and keep my emotional distance. I have weathered much and we must live on.

***I need to add that here in this life, after my son's death, I seem to lose purpose. I just go through the motions of providing and tending to my children. I become distant towards my husband, almost as if I am blaming him… or is it that I am distancing myself because I think that he blames me?

In this lifetime, I "see" and understand how I use my "tight upper lip" and my tough upright stance to really hold on to myself, to control my reactions as to not allow my emotions to show, feeling that if my emotions reach the surface, I will not be able to control them and hence some unnecessary harm might arise because of my lack of self-discipline and rationality for which I will never forgive myself. As I write this, I cry from down deep inside of my soul, lamenting my son's death, my ego, my lack of wisdom and an overall disgust in how I handle the situation. My detachment was due to not trusting myself to ever overreact again. Wow!!! Someone remind me to do a healing on this lifetime to alleviate my soul from this anguish and despair.

The Count of Anjou (I just love these pears, really, I do!!)

Time: Late 1000's
Location: Present Day, Anjou, France and Middle East
The true First Crusade

I was a count, and glad to be part of a very unique and important expedition. My cousins shared with me this "opportunity". My cousins and I would visit with one another's families often, to hang out, go hunting and of course, to check out the people staying in town. Our families were devout Catholics. Anything for the Pope!!! It was now time to prove our manhood, our knightly ways and our loyalty to the Her Almighty Catholic Church. Even family members, either by blood or married in, from today Scotland joined this wonderful and proud adventure, for we were now to be the protectors of the people during their journeys to the Holy Land.

I was young, either in my late teens to mid-twenties. One thing that I knew for sure was that I was a very moral young man with high ideals. My cousins and I embarked, saddled with wines, breads and salted and smoked meats of all sorts. In every town we travelled through, we were received like kings and respectively ate like ones also. Every principality that we stayed in had a trinket or two to be blessed and coins to support the cause. As we travelled further east and south, the food changed, with more spices and less heavy meats.

We had fun, playing pranks on one another, horse-riding competition, and how many ribbons we could collect from the damsels. It is a trip, an adventure that I shall never regret and always relish deep in my soul of true brotherly camaraderie. It didn't matter if one of us was from across the waters to the west nor south past the tips of the mountain ridges. We were a brotherhood, which I honoured with all my soul, even to this present day, 2000's AD lifetime. It is as if we recognize one another's soul and are true to one another.

I had a couple of comrades that I was exceptionally close with, an in-law from today's Scotland and another cousin who was my age, a tad bit younger. I always had their backs. I even raised one of their son's… which I shall go into detail later.

We travelled across land and then boat. As we travelled further east, at times we came across some hostilities with the believers of Islam. We intended always to be peaceful though stern, and at times we had to diligently protect our civilian travelers so that they may complete their pilgrimage to the Holy Land. We also had our prayer times.

Upon arriving to the eastern lands, after several years, there were more than a few battles that we were involved with to protect the rights of the Holy Land. It seems that the children of Judaism and the followers of Islam were always on attack with one another. I never understood this needless need of religious superiority to honour the same High God, tsk, tsk, tsk. (To me it all sounded the same, except in the customary way in honouring our God.) We won our battles and due to this, the Jewish leaders offered us a location to call our own.

Here at our own fort, we were offered cultural tutors and servants. I roomed with my Scottish in-law. He was an important man, back in his land. He was tall and strong, had red hair and a catchy gregarious laugh, that just tempted you to laugh with him no matter the subject line. He had a wife back home. He was very interested in the eastern science that he was learning from our tutors. He was also very fond of a certain important servant from a rich family that he fawned over.

During our stay, I learned about the different fruits that were such a delicacy to us westerners. The spices, grains and meat, you would not believe, that just melted in your mouth. I thought that us Catholics were devout, the whole area would stop several times a day to pray and we were expected to respect the ritual with silence. They had an intense music with beautiful sounding instruments and the women wore colours I hadn't seen before. There were exotic birds that didn't fly and trees filled, all year round with some kind of fruit and even indoors. The buildings had unique designs and the interior was such I hadn't seen before, far from the simplicity of my homeland.

The people knew so much, the stars, the numbers, cooking and health. We felt like naïve children among these people, even the commoners knew so much, we were just some uncouth brutes to many of them. And then she came to be our personal servant, the daughter of a prominent family. She taught and guided us on many topics, and my Scots comrade tutored her on the lessons of the flesh. They had an affair until the day he left, which was about a couple of years before I did. When he left, she was pregnant, yet never revealed this to him and kept it from her family. She confided in me as a true friend of her lover. She raised her little boy in the complex, away from her family's knowledge... until one day, someone realized the boy was her child.

Her brothers and father came storming in demanding to see the little boy, we had hid him in a huge vassal and when she told them that he had died recently the eldest brother still killed her for she had brought such shame to the family. As soon as I could, I fled with the boy, travelling back to France and then to Scotland to introduce him to his father. He could not deny him. Even though the boy had dark skin, he had green eyes and red hair such as his father. During the whole travels I cared, raised and taught the boy as my own. I had loved his mother dearly, I had been in love with her, but due to the respect for my comrade I never approached her with intimacy.

After my Scots friend had left, she and I continued our tutoring and sharing of knowledge. She had a beautiful smile where her eyes lit up, soft curls that trimmed her face and a beautiful caramel colouring of skin. She always smelled so enticing and relaxing. I do believe that the whole compound was in love with her.

When I arrived in Scotland, I noticed that my friend's wife was now pregnant. She was our family member and if they found out that she was cheated on, then he no longer will carry his prominent post. He couldn't keep the boy, so I took him back with me to Anjou, and raised him as my own. As the boy grew, he learned and spoke several languages and became an important courier between countries as far east as the Holy Land and as far west as Scotland. I was very proud of him and loved him as my own son.

I believe that I returned to the Holy Land later and died there. I know that I was important in international matters.

I learned in this lifetime, that family is who you make of it, one can never know everything, everyone deserves love, all religions have validity towards happiness as long as no harm is done, life is always an adventure and love is precarious yet the most beautiful feeling one can experience.

**A side note. So, at the time that I "saw" this life, I wasn't aware that light eyes and red hair originated in the Middle East. So, in hindsight, perhaps when I had gone to Scotland to deliver my comarade's son, and thinking that it was obvious that the boy was his, might really be a cycle where my red-headed comrade had returned to his own deep roots. Ideas that make you go, ...hmmmm?".

Native Medicine Woman

Location: Fairbanks Park area, Costa Mesa, Ca, Catalina Island & Ventura County, California
Time Period: 1200's
Gender: female
Lived till: about 65's

I really like parts of this lifetime. To this day Catalina Island has a special place in my soul. In this day and age, I enjoy just hanging out on the beach, staring off in the distance. Catalina Island is my quick escape. I even enjoy just the journey across the waters over there, the crisp freshness of her waters, the abundance of herbs and the fresh breeze that she receives from all sides of the island.

So, in this lifetime, I am a medicine woman, brought up in a medicine family. We would travel back and forth, across the waters between today, Southern California, the Channel Islands and Catalina Island. I can see us paddling in the canoes and my medicinal hut. I "see" myself looking off from the cliffs towards Catalina Island, I called it my Mother's land. I could tell by the winds when it was the best time to paddle over there. And when we did, we did it as a group, taking several canoes together. It was a whole day journey and we would eat dried meat and any fish we caught for the journey. The dolphins would accompany us on our journey, being our guardians. At times we would see whales and sharks. When we would see sharks, we would join our canoes together to make them believe that we were a bigger fish than they were. On rare occasions we would see orcas, then we knew that something was off, for it wasn't often, not even yearly that we would see orcas. It was quite scary for they would attack and bump the canoes, they weren't serene like the whales.

I travelled back and forth from the mainland to the island many times a year since my childhood with my family and later with my own family. It was always such an adventure. We would trade and harvest herbs for me to take back to the mainland. I kind of had my own little "residence" on the island for I came often and stayed from anywhere from one week to two months at a time. I also came at times just to get some peace, meditate and rejuvenate.

My people and I ate a lot of food from the sea, nuts, seeds and small animals.

I was the main healer, having inherited the honour from my father. I cherished this position and the coastal people of many tribes knew me and I would travel far to help others. I would sing/chant as I made the concoctions of teas and tinctures giving thanks to MotherLand for her gifts. I would travel up the coastline, all the way to today Pt Magu to down south San Diego, bringing my healing herbs and helping the people.

I was "married" to a man, I was his second wife. His first wife had died from Pneumonia, due to drowning. He had two children with her. We had for sure at least one child together. We were a family of five. His first born died before us, having fallen against a rock. My husband was the tribal historian, where he would teach the history of our people and paint our history on the skins of animals. My present day son, Wolf, was our child.

Several times my husband would take us on long journeys that took a year or two, deep into the lands, away from my precious waters. He had family there. I didn't care for it, for it was too hot and I would miss the energies of my waters. Yet, out of respect for my husband I would go. In time, I learned to enjoy myself, a bit, reluctantly, realizing it did me no good to be resentful. My "sisters", actually, his sisters, would make it all worth it and fun.

When I first married, my husband and I were very good friends. He was outgoing, interactive with both me and the children. He was jovial. As time passed, and I mean about ten years later, he seems to start to obviously slow down, to become disinterested in the tribal affairs, cynical and depressed. I slowly separate me and the children from him, becoming more involved with healing and travelling to acquire the herbs. It is as if he became resentful towards me, though I am not sure for what, perhaps my youth? I do know that it didn't bring me down, I continued as a medicine woman, even though my husband didn't want my help.

In this lifetime, I am aware that I am not my husband's love of his life, that it was his first wife, yet I respect my culture's tradition of a woman "needing" to marry and produce children. Though I love my children dearly and in gratitude for them, I was not in so much need of a passionate love affair for my deep passion was for the herbs and the elements, Mother Nature. I had tried to help my husband even though I was not a submissive wife to him. As he became older, he became more needy and wanted to be catered to and not try to heal himself. This was not my philosophy nor lifestyle, so I didn't indulge him.

My husband died some ten years before I did, in some kind of accident. I lived until I was about 65 years of age. I died content and at peace with my life, with my children and tribe members by my side. I was sent drifting away for the whales to take me to the Great White Spirit.

Angolian Captured Slave Woman

Time period: Early 1500s African Slave
Location: West Africa, Angola and the Atlantic Ocean
Gender: Female
Age: 16yrs
Warning: sexual graphics**

I "see" myself, Black, short hair, topless, on a wooden floor, made to pleasure three-four black men who also have chains on. I do not want to do it. The men slaves tell me to or that the filthy sick devils will kill us. I have a thick metal band around my neck, hands and ankles. I do not want to do this. I do not even know what it is I am supposed to do. The big black man tells me to just do as he says and he will protect me. The filthy white sick devils watch, give instructions and laugh. Why do I have to do this? I do not want to put this big man's dong in my mouth or touch it with my tongue or hands!!! Why did they pick me? The floor rocks, we are in a rocking shed and I feel all alone. I want my family, my village and now I have no safety. I get slapped and spanked, on my breasts and ass, like a beast when I do not know what to do. I try to listen to my fellow male slaves, but I never have done what they want me to do and do not know why I should. The filthy white dirty hairy devils tell the men to do things, to touch me in areas that they do not know why either. They just want to rut me like a pig, but the filthy devils tell them to touch me between my legs, to choke me with their dongs, to stab me like a pig. I am ashamed. I am scared and ashamed, not just for myself but also for my fellow captives. We just want to arrive safely. Will we? And what is there when we arrive? Will we be treated better?

I get used every day. Every day the same thing. Now I think that my fellow male captives look forward to this. Sometimes it can feel good, I am ashamed. The big captive always stabs me first from behind, I do not know why. He says so that way everyone knows that I am his. Why am I his? Why am I not me? Sometimes the dirty devils have me used several times a day to give a show. My protector is always with me, he is kind, stern, demanding, always first and always protective of me, nevertheless he took me as his own and I was then made to give life to other slaves.

As time goes by, while we are on this rocking shed, I get taken upstairs to see the sky and waters, this is where groups of the filthy devils watch me being taken by my protector and other slaves, we are their show. My tummy keeps getting bigger, it is not because I have eaten a lot, in fact, we are practically starved. My protector says that it is proof that I am his, because he always takes me first.

I do not know where we are going. I do not know, no longer, who I am. This torment has been long, many days, I no longer get my womanhood, for a while, my tummy grows, I suffocate in the rocking shed with all the other captives. This is not life! This is not right! This rocking shed is ruled by white filthy stinky gross devils! Other women captives tell me that I am with a baby. No!! I can't be, not here, not with these filths, not without my village.

I reminisce about my family and recall the day the other village captures us and the longing of sadness in my father's eyes. I was his favourite ceremonial dancer, to have captured me was to take the luck away from my village. We walked far, long and towards the big waters. Now, I am no longer me, no longer special, just a beast.

I am brought out to the open air, on top of the rocking shed. Just water as far as I can see. Only filthy white devils on top and my few fellow captives who will use me again as laughs for the devils. I do not want to. I won't. I yell that I won't. I get hit by the devil, I do not care. I look at my black men and yell no and I jump. I jump with metal bands on my ankles, wrists and neck and I do not care. I land in the water and start to fall down deeper. It is so blue, so dark, I give in. I am free, me and my baby are free.

This lifetime affected me so much as I "saw" it, the pain, despair, confusion, no rhyme no reason, the repugnance of what was going on and my surroundings and feelings of disconnection from my family, home and everything that I ever knew was being drowned and flushed out of me. If this is life, this is a nightmare in which I wanted nothing to do with it. I try to "see" if there was any karma and purpose of this lifetime and at this time I cannot "see" any, which saddens me to think that it might have been a waste of a life yet I have no idea how my life, then, might have affected other's karma and purposes.

After I wrote this, I shared this lifetime with my husband and son. I cried intensely as I read this to them, and shortly after, I even threw up, mostly phlegm, nevertheless, I did. There was a lot of healing I had to do. I even did some Ho'oponopono with my soul.

Daughter of a Basque Whaler

Time period: 1500s
Location: Basque Region
Nationality: Basque
Gender: Female
Died: young from a sickness

The first scene I had with this lifetime, was seeing me at an open market selling fish and oil. My family were basque whalers and we, my mother and I, were used to not seeing my eldest brother and father for long periods of time due to their fishing exploits, which took them as far away as northern Canada. Now, I have to interject here, that there are many scenes that I just can't believe what I am "seeing" due to my lack of history knowledge of certain locations and time periods. So, I remember that when I was "seeing" I was confused…and it is not the first time that that happens, where I am doubting what I am "seeing" though I just go with the flow…

Back to the scene… I can smell the sea, we have shells and all sorts of whale oil soap (I am shaking my head, because I turned to my husband as I write this saying, "How does my soul know this? I don't even know that soap was made from whale oil. Of course, my soul knows, it lived it! Hahaha"). My mother is meandering about, talking with the other market people. I have my little brother/sister with me (because I see a younger sister/brother, though maybe it is a cousin my mother is caring for. I only know that the younger child is blond with hair to its shoulders and light soft curls at the ends). I was about nine or ten years of age and with a lot of responsibility.

So, I am at our stand talking with a customer about how fresh and wonderful our soaps are, when low and behold, a young man, scares me from behind that I grabbed a fish, turned around and slapped him with it! It was my older brother who had just returned from one of his expeditions. I loved him dearly. Since, my father died when I was barely born or very young I am not quite sure from what, due to the younger child that I "see" with me. I looked up to my brother as the father figure, a male figure that I could trust. My mother relied on him very much, especially when he was in between expeditions. She would visit her family, out and up in the hills, for a week or two upon my brother's arrival, where they made a different variety of dairy products. She would always return with a lot of dairy products which we then sold also with our whale oil products. I have a sneaky suspicion that she doesn't only visit my uncle, but also a "special" friend, she is a widow, so it is okay.

(I notice that certain views, perspectives and phrasing of thoughts as I see" have much to do with the age and experience in which I have had at the time of the scene).

My brother and mother worked hard to take care of our family. My mother is such a talker, so very friendly with everyone and everybody loves her. My older brother, whose name starts with an E sound, just rolls his eyes at her. I have a sister who is older than I am and is already married off, meaning, we hardly see her. She is about 14-15 years of age. I also had a younger sibling. My older brother was very buddy-buddy with our cousin who also was a whaler, you know, family business.

There is another scene where my cousin returns from an expedition without my brother. He is in charge of relating the inconsolable bad news that my brother went overboard and drowned. They couldn't get him in time. I am devastated. My cousin ends up being my mother's right hand and helps her run the family business. The death of my brother affects my mother deeply, she ages overnight.

The last scene I recall is of me dying. It is about a year or two after my brother's death, and I have some kind of flu, pneumonia, or tuberculosis. I see myself pale, coughing a lot and it hurts. In fact, it seems that the cold sea air makes it worse, though I feel stifled and need air. I can see the sadness in my younger sibling's eyes and heart. My cousin tries to comfort me, and my mother is distant. She is there but doesn't interact much with me. Either she doesn't know what to do or she is protecting herself emotionally because of the previous deaths that she has dealt with already. I feel so badly for my mother, I have a feeling ripping at my heart, feeling so badly that I cannot take care of my mother. She has no one anymore. My father and brother, both have died, my sister is gone, married somewhere, and now I too am leaving her. I feel helpless, destitute of life for her. I wish she would come to me, I am slipping away. I am not angry, I just worry that she won't know that I love her. My cousin gives me a shot of some strong alcohol, I close my eyes, and I dream. I am no longer with my family, I am floating, floating and floating. I never see my family again.

Some lifetimes I "see" clearly what my life purpose and karma are, though this lifetime, it seems that my purpose and karma is to enjoy the family unity and love when it is around. Some people may feel that a purpose has to relate to a drive to accomplish something out of the ordinary, forgetting that keeping the family together and being the emotional support system are important purposes also, and maybe that was my karma, for perhaps in a past life, I had separated us.

Wife of a Hawaiian Chief

Time Period: 1620's-1645
Location: Hawaii
Gender: Female
Husband: Rayray, 10 years older
Children: total of 6, three died before the age of 10 years: Aris, Becky and Sophie, living are Wolf, Gaby and Alejandro

Astrological Influence: Jupiter in 6Aries, Saturn in 17Gemini (present life Nessus same degree and sign), Uranus in 26Cancer (my present life Sun's degrees and sign), Neptune in 14Libra, Pluto in 10Taurus, North Node in 4Capricorn, Chiron in 28Aquarius.

I was from the present island of Maui, my husband, a Kahuna, was from the Big Island. He was about 10 years older than I was. We married when I was about 15 years of age. During our life together, another 10 years, we had a total of 6 children (boy oh boy, smh, hahaha), three did die for one reason or another, two before the age of 10 years and a baby died in a hurricane before the age of three years.

My husband loved me dearly, he treasured me like a precious jewel. He called me his Malaikai. He was a good leader, well respected and loved by his people. We went out often on canoes to travel around the islands. He had cousins who were leaders of other areas and islands. He held ceremonies often, at the waterfall, full moon, new moon, when certain birds flew by, when mammals swam by at the beginning of a "season" and when he noticed a change in the weather. He traveled according to the birds and mammals. He interacted much with his children, had them with him as much as possible.

So, several scenes stand out, here goes the first scene…

There is a huge storm, hurricane in process going steadily stronger and stronger. I am going around tying my children to trees to protect them. The winds are so strong that my almost 3-years of age son is ripped from my hand and I cannot get to him in time before he is thrown against a rock, dies instantly and is drifted off into the ocean by the storm tide. I am so torn to go to his limp body and from helping my other children. As I tie myself to a tree, holding another child, crying, I see the water coming and pulling his body out to sea, to never be seen again. I cry every time I "see" this scene, and believe it or not, this is the second time that I write this on my computer and it tears at my heart. I guess that I didn't save it the first time. That baby that I lost is my present life husband of now. Each time that

I have written this, on paper and computer, he, my present day husband, consoles me and reminds me that we are together now. This is one of my past life scenes that just "kills me inside". After I finish writing about this lifetime, for sure, I am doing an energy clearing.

Moving on, there is another scene, where my husband, children, village people and I take off to another island… a volcanic eruption is due to occur and we are all now hiding out in caves on a distant island with our food supply for a while. The skies turn night time with bright lights, it is a battle of the stars going on, this is how we explain it to the children. The ancestors are fighting for rights to the lands. Soon after the volcanic eruption comes swells of ocean walls coming towards the island where we are. We end up staying in the caves, high up in the lands, for a total of four days, to protect ourselves and our food from the ashes. It was a fascinating time, just a tad bit scary, for our people are used to volcanic eruptions, they are our gods, our fertilizer for the land and our destruction if not respected.

The next scene is also a sad one for me, I lose my dear and beloved husband. My husband has had issues with an uncle who is just a big asshole, though he is not at all as tall as my husband, though about the same age. He attacks my husband's side of the island from another island. There is absolutely no reason for him to attack and want our side, he doesn't even have issues on our island, yet there is this unwanted rivalry, because my husband's uncle's father keeps openly comparing his son to my husband and making his son feel less of a man, which then the uncle starts to hate my husband who hasn't done anything to his uncle.

I detested this man, he caused unnecessary malaise in our lives and fear in my children's eyes. In the past, my husband and the village people have victoriously battled the uncle and his men off the island, but not this time. My husband has been lamed from a spear to his hip from one of their past quarrels and now he is not as strong. He loses this battle and his cheap shot taker uncle wins.

My husband's uncle has a big ceremony where he is to assassinate my husband, in front of me and my children, besides the village people. At least, he also gives an elaborate funeral ceremony, upon my insistence, because now I am to be his (the uncle's) wife, reluctantly, and as a wedding gift, I ask for my precious beloved husband's proper funeral ceremony where both my children and I can grieve.

During our marriage I am cold, reluctant and nonphysically responsive and because of that he rapes me each time, yet never is able to impregnate me, hmmm.

I live for only another three years. I haven't yet "seen" why I die, but after having been with this "new husband", I really do not mind.

In this lifetime, I have a deep sense of family, romantic love, a sense of responsibility to my village besides family and towards the end...disgust. Before I remarried in my present life, I would go back to this lifetime to show and remind me what true love is, which helped me to open myself up and allow myself what love is in my present life. I am thankful that I can revisit my past lives when I am feeling lost to guide forward. I am also thankful to my beautiful family of this lifetime in Hawai'i for that deep love.

Japan 1644

Location: Present day Japan
Time period: 1644
Gender: Female
Children: at least one, Wolf, boy
Died at about 40 years of age

Astrological Influence: Jupiter in 15Aries-24Taurus, Uranus in Scorpio, North Node in 19Virgo-2Virgo (present life South Node degrees and sign), Neptune 2Sagittarius, Pluto 3Gemini, Saturn 2Aries-14Aries

In this lifetime, I am a wife of a daimyo in Northern Japan. I have a lover and a son from this lover though my husband thinks it is his. I am trained as a ninja, Kunoichi, due to family influence.

My husband as a daimyo travels often and always takes his first wife. I was left behind to ensure the "education", "the ways of us", which included calligraphy, physical abilities, our philosophies of spirituality and female etiquette. I recall that I played an instrument, almost equivalent to an ukulele. I loved my spiritual garden and the smell of the vegetables growing. The trees would tell me when there was trouble in the air. We ate mostly seafood and noodles. Sometimes we did eat pork, it was a delicacy and ceremonial.

Our home was set on fire from an enemy. My lover, a ninja of our court and father of my son, helps us to escape through an underground tunnel, then to Hokkaido, and then across the sea to now Korea. In Korea, I taught females to be ninjas and my son grew to be a samurai.

I died by having my head chopped off. I cannot tell if it was a seppuku with the help of a fast death by the chopping off of my head.

The scene that first came to me when I was "seeing" was the fire and my lover scurrying us away to an underground tunnel as the fire gets closer and closer to us. He and several others are with us and lead us out of the tunnel and clandestinely to Hokkaido.

The next scene is again where we are fleeing from Hokkaido, a few years later, for we are still being searched and I no longer want to be found by my husband nor the enemy family. We eventually settle in what is now South Korea. In this small town, I help the people to develop, become more cultured and to defend themselves.

In this lifetime, there is a sense that I am often hiding my true identity, not just in name but also in abilities. Even as a child, I had to hide the true fact of who my father really was. Also in this life I try to help the people of the area, (no matter where I am) almost creating a type of "school", but not officially. Every day I shared a different topic. I felt that all knowledge should be universal.

My last thoughts, "Though I lived in extreme fear, I am very glad to share with the people, there is extreme satisfaction that I have fulfilled my life purpose in this lifetime. I have no regrets except to have been able to have had more time with my lover and my son. But it is time and I know it and accept it willingly, I leave you all with love."

In this lifetime I have a sense of accomplishment, courage, integrity and honour that in all that I did, I respected myself and no one could take that away from me even if I was to behave a certain way and be with particular people. My sense of dignity was always intact.

Late 1600's, about 1688, I was born.

Time period: late 1600's, about 1688
Gender: male
Location: Canada
Father: present day grandfather
Nationality: French
Died: 1730
Siblings: older sister and younger step-sister
Mother: Fille-du-Roi, died of typhus

The first scene is that I am watching my father, side view, a way down, sitting on the porch, making some honey or maple peach whiskey, while I was working on our pig farm. We raised pigs, made whiskey and smoked the pork also. I can smell the scents as I write this lifetime, the pork, the sweet peaches and the maple trees. I loved my family who were my parents, my older sister and me. My mother gave birth to a total of four babies before she died when I was 13 years of age. I was happy, safe and secure. We worked hard but it was well worth it, and in my mind, we were happy as a family. My father loved my mother and never made her feel badly for being an orphan, on the contrary, he loved her deeply. Then my mother contracted typhus and died. He was devastated and my older sister took to taking care of us.

My father remarried about 12 years later to a hungry money bitch of a wife, who was a widow and already had a daughter a few years younger than myself, like 7 years. The daughter was a brat, what she saw, she demanded and her ridiculous mother gave it to her. I wasn't too keen on my step-mother nor my step-sister. I couldn't understand why my dad remarried, I thought that we were doing just fine. And boy oh boy, did those two women stir up a hornet's nest. (I guess, looking back, a man doesn't want to die alone. Hm)

So the second scene, which I "saw" was when I remet this soul, my step-sister's soul in this present life. (At first, I am always thrilled to reencounter a past life soul, and then, reality hits, hahaha). It was with such endearment that I met her (she is female in this life), I was instinctively and instantaneously protective of her. So in the past life, I was a very naughty young man. We had a party at my dad's home, (I lived on the property but not in the same house, you know, young man wants his privacy and it was a kind of man cave for me and my buddies), my dad and his wife were not there. We all got a bit drunk, okay, very drunk. It seems, (you notice that I use this phrasing when I, myself, from this present life time is still in either shock or awe of what is going on)… that somehow, my step-sister and I ended up in her bedroom and made out and I felt her up, somehow it all stopped and I went downstairs. The next day, I acted as if nothing had happened, and nor did she ever acknowledge or even drop a hint that she remembered what had happened. I guess as a man, I was feeling "whew!" Later on when she started dating my buddy from that lifetime, I was not thrilled at all, not out of envy, but out of caution because I knew what a womanizer he was and a frequenter of the brothels.

Now, this leads to the next scene where I hear something like an explosion or a very loud noise, from my area of the property. I climb out of my window onto the roof and I see my dad's house up in flames and my step-sister with my "buddy" running out all drunk, but not necessarily in fear but out of a type of laughter, like oops, hahaha, what did we do, hahaha. All I know is that my blood sister wasn't there, and my father was on the property in our distillery. I had to go run in and pull out my step mother. My step-sister and her boyfriend had been drinking and must have knocked over a candle or two in their sloppiness, and that is what started the fire. Half of the house burned down. (what is neat to say is that in this present lifetime, my "step sister" from the Canadian lifetime is very good at managing money, so her soul has also learned a lesson).

I love to "see" my past lives. It is an on-going soap opera, entertaining, and eye-opening lessons. This past life showed me why I am so protective of my grandfather and that deep connection that I feel for him. (We should remember that connections are not always reciprocal.) It also showed me yet another lifetime where I am fond of pork. Before becoming Vegan, I was such a pork-eater. I never was a real big fan of beef, but I did love my pork and seafood. By the way, did I mention how much I used to love pork, hahaha. Now-a-days, piggies are safe around me. In fact, I wouldn't mind owning one as a pet for they are really smart animals.

"Seeing" this past life also enlightened me about my slight fear of leaving candles unattended and on during the night. It seems that watching our home go up in smoke carried through to this lifetime and I am very vigilant with candles.

Martinique 1700's

Gender: male
Birthdate: 1735
Location: the Island of Martinique
Race: creole
Mother: My Omi, Anne-Marie, was my mother
Father:
Younger sister:

It seems that the 1700's had a lot of French influence, perhaps it explains my ease with the language in this lifetime even though it is my fourth language and not a native nor blood language.

I remember that when I was "seeing" all the scenes, I was quite perplexed, obviously due to my lack of historical knowledge of Martinique, slaves in the Caribbean and the Creoles. I was quite surprised at the fact that my family were slave owners, speaking French and that our family was originally from Africa. As I was "seeing" I was in shock, feeling badly as a mixed race woman of the late 1900's. This is when I really learned to separate my present self from my past lives and not to judge my soul for its past being and choices. It seems that I was also related to Napoleon's Josephine somehow, hopefully it will come to me before I finish this book. (As I am editing this book, I have yet "seen" the connection.)

This was a fun life, young, male, creole, from a well to do family with clout, who travelled a few times to both France and French Canada, exporting and importing from Martinique. One of my best buddies was my present day son, Wolfgang. He was also a male in this past life, younger than I was, full white French and as mischievous as ever (of course, I am going to say that…I am his present day mother, hahaha). Boy oh boy, did I and my buddy have fun and oh wait, I was also married to a gorgeous creole wife.

So, I had both an older and younger sister, and we grew up on our sugar plantation. My younger sister was chronically sick, and after doing military service in the French Navy, I brought my mother and both sisters with me to France. Unfortunately, my younger sister ended up dying before turning 15 years of age. I was let out of the French Navy service due to an incident where I "fell", pushed into a pool of cement by an envious French officer who felt that I was unworthy of my "bought" post. This is where Wolf comes in… he pulls me out of the pool of drying cement and he and another officer start hammering the cement off me.

Before I continue, the first scene I "saw" was a bit before July 4th, 2017 and I was detoxing from Breast Cancer and my son, Wolfgang, was resting by my side on the bed with me. I had nodded off when all of a sudden I heard what I thought were cannons. I started talking to Wolf, saying "I hear the cannons but I do not know what side we are on…the French or the Spanish?" Wolf replied to me in a haze, saying, "French". Then I realized I had been "seeing" and Wolf had taken off with me to previous dimensions. (He naturally travels and takes off quite quickly) but what I thought was so cool was that Wolf answered in his half sleepy state… "French" and that he was right. His soul was connected. In this scene, Wolf, my French buddy, and I are riding horses away from the "fort" and we hear cannons and decide to take refuge a bit further away by some trees. We were carrying an important message.

The next scene I "saw" was sometime later, but due to the surroundings I recalled which past life it was. I was walking up towards a huge white house, my white father was there and my creole mother, and off to the side was my creole wife, who was wearing gold with a brown diamond pattern dress. She was lovely. Now, this scene for me in this lifetime is very important, because I was "seeing" this scene as who I am now, a heterosexual woman, yet, when I saw my wife of that life time, I genuinely felt a deep romantic love for her and sexual attraction. I felt my heart fill up with the warmth of a growing glow just spreading through me. All I kept thinking is that I was so in love with my wife and in great gratitude for the children she had bore me. After coming back to this lifetime, I had a renewed faith in love and what love really felt like, and this was really important at that time because this was a couple of years before getting together with my husband. I was divorced, gone through a few sexual relationships yet not really aware of knowing what is a true love affair. Having had returned to the lifetime in Martinique showed me what love really feels like and not these superficial sexual attractions that I had encountered in the past. Have I encountered my wife from Martinique in this lifetime? Yes, oh yes, and she is a male for whom I have a deep respect and I do know that in this lifetime, we are here to support one another not be in a romantic relationship.

Yes, yes there are more scenes, many more. This is a lifetime in which I probably have "seen" the most. I had scenes where I am leaving Martinique with barrels of sugar loaded on a ship, a buque. Scenes where I leave a port of France and sail to Canada before going to Martinique, doing many trades.

Then there are several scenes that take place in Louisiana. One in particular where I have to laugh, as I am watching this…okay, so Wolf, who is my French buddy is frolicking around with all these women openly, low and behold, I "see" ourselves in a brothel. It appears that I am doing the finance books and Wolf is indulging in good wine, pastries and luscious well-endowed women who are fawning all over him (they have no idea that he is penniless, me and my family take care of him; he is my sidekick and my right hand). He is living the life and my mother doesn't quite mind because Wolf sure is a charmer.

I indulged in his every whim, not so much just for having saved my life back in France when I fell in a pool of cement, but also for always being there. I was not only indebted to him, I endeared him truly. He helped me move on, past my humiliation of being pushed in the cement pool and the separation with my wife, and not ever seeing my children again. He was like the little brother I never had, and for whatever reason, he was completely content, following me around from France to Canada down to Louisiana and I was thankful. And indulgent he was. He died young, of syphilis, probably from one of our girls, or many of our girls, back then who knows.

He became very concerned and self-conscious about his gorgeous face, even going blind. (It is interesting because in this life time, he does have a very keen interest on "clean" sex and concerns of being blind.)

One day, a beautiful day, I found him on the side of the road, having fallen from his horse. It was too late, he was already dead. I am so sadden, grief-stricken with an immense sense of guilt and loss, "why did I let him go by himself?!" "what am I going to do without him?" All I know is that it was during the American Revolution, though we weren't fighting in the 7-year war either. We had constructed our brothel/pastry shop before the wars. I was in my 40's or barely when he died. As I write this, I am crying deeply, releasing all the anguish of his death from that lifetime.

Okay, let's back it up (and do remember, hahaha, past life pun, that I have not "seen" in chronological order, so there are jumping back and forth quite a lot), after my father's death back in Martinique, we sold the plantation, I moved my mother to Louisiana (my other sister died back in France), my other sister stayed in Canada, must have been a man involved, for back then, that would be the only reason a girl would separate from her mother. That is when we had bought and/or constructed the brothel/pastry shop where I ran the accounts upstairs. My mother who was only 17 years older than myself had died before me. I died at the age of 45 years, protecting one of my brothel girls. The inheritance of the brothel/pastry shop went to my sister, back in Canada.

I just loved this life, though there was pain, I felt truly as a man who honoured his responsibilities and was very proud of it. I had made a deep and wonderful friendship with Wolf, I had loved a beautiful woman (even though I lost her to another back in France and my children, and because they were girls it was easier to bear. I know, I know, how sexist…I was a man in the 1700's, what more could I say?

I also realized that my present day Omi, had been my mother in a couple of lives. I have a deep attachment to her, so much that I still talk to her almost daily on the "other side".

Prussian Soldier

Time period: Late 1700's-1815ish, I was a Prussian soldier...
Gender: male
Location: Prussia
Died: in my mid-twenties
My Apa, Rafael, was my father

One of my step-uncles was my sister, his husband's sister was an acquaintance of ours in this lifetime, where in this past life, I had a crush on him, who was back then a her. I gave her a 24k gold and amber necklace, it was a promise to marry me upon returning from the war.

My mother, Baerbel, was my commanding officer and a really good friend of Rafael. She was Adav Georg von Agthe.

So, in this lifetime I was a handsome, yet frail man of early twenties, more of a student, an academia than a soldier about to go off to the Patriotic War of 1812, under the command of my father's good friend as his secretary due to my expansive education. My mother wasn't too keen on me going off to war, it seems that I was frail due to some asthma or something that she didn't allow me to be very active outdoors. My father felt that she was just too overprotective and it was time for me to prove my manhood, ugh!

I do have a deep connection to my mother in this lifetime. Every time my father left on military business, I was her confidant, her partner and her best friend. We would play cards together, go into town together, meet and receive her friends together and of course, eat our meals together. So, it is obvious how she was overly protective of me, not just because I was her only son, but I took the place of my father when he was absent, which was often and for days to weeks at a time.

***This is an excerpt from the recording I did when I was cancer detoxing. "I am just me, not what you wanted. I know that you despise me. I am sorry that I am just me. I know that I embarrass you. I just want to leave your presence because you despise my presence. I am sorry that I cannot be what you wanted." This is from the lifetime when I was a son of a General from the Napoleonic Wars. In that lifetime, my father was a general and it seems that I had an illness or weakness that affected my immune system at a very young age, and somehow I also broke my leg. My father in that lifetime felt that my mother coddled me too much and I would play board games and cards with her, and she would have me read to her.

I had two younger siblings and at least one or two older siblings also. My older siblings and father thought that I was a loser. I felt solace being around my mother. Eventually my father sent me to a military academy where I excelled in education, books and strategies.

Physically, I was just average. I did excel and graduate with honors due to my academic abilities.

I ended up going to war. I really didn't like wars. Because this was such an important role, my father wanted to have the pride that his only son was partaking in this war. His officership was at such a high level, if I did well, he would even advance more for just having produced a worthy and honourable son…but, I didn't know how to fight, shoot a rifle, fence or fight with a sword, though I could mount and ride a horse quickly. Again, I do not really know what I was "sick" with or that my mother just used it as an excuse to keep me near her.

So, going back to the initial scene, I arrive back at the post and I see my commanding officer, Baerbel, down, bleeding from the chest, right in front of our tent. I was intensely scared, I tried to pick him up, but he said, "no". I remember just thinking that I was going to be in so much shit. I felt very very guilty, repeating to myself, I am just a secretary, I am just a secretary, I am not made for this. I felt that I let down my commanding officer, by having stepped away from the tent (I had to go give a message to another officer), that I let down my father and the whole army.

The following scene, something had happened to my leg again. I am in crutches with a bandage on my head. I recall it was from an explosion.

In the next scene, I am walking into my family's ballroom. (did I mention that my family had a huge home? One of those with a twirling staircase and huge chandelier, with at least one maid, butler and a chef, and a stable. We were really well off, I was tutored for the most part of my life and so was my younger sister.) There was an elegant gathering occurring, men in military dress uniforms and women in elaborate ball gowns, dressed to the nine. As I walked in, my father sees me, he has had several drinks already, he walks towards me in a stiffen angry manner and condemns me in front of all the guests, telling me how worthless I am, how I should be ashamed of myself and I was an embarrassment to the family name and then he back-handed me. I was hurt, my pride was disgraced. It hurt me so much that he despised me in such a manner that he would slap me in front of everybody. I felt worthless, I felt like a loser. I felt like I was just some kind of nerd who could do nothing else. I hated my dad for embarrassing me and not loving me, nor supporting me after everything that I had tried to do so that he could be proud of me. He didn't care. I wanted to hit back and I wanted to die at the same time. All I could do was just stand there until he walked away. Out of sheer humiliation, I ran out of the "palace" to the stables, took a horse and rode it into town. I went to a small tavern and started drinking away my life. I felt that I could never live it down, I never returned home. I had returned to the war and about two and a half weeks later, I shot myself in the mouth in a drunken stupor, committing suicide, leaving my family an apology letter of the type of worthless son I was. Though because it was at a battle where I committed suicide, my family didn't have to lose face because of it. I had just drunk myself pathetic, feeling that there was no way that I could continue to live through this humiliation, that I had no right to marry my fiancée, and that I had no right to exist.

I can see how in this lifetime, while my biological parents were still married, how I really tried to make them proud of me. In this life, I strove to not just be academic yet also an athlete, tried to be able to be independent, and for the longest I had a deep need to protect my mother Baerbel, who had been that dying commanding officer in my arms. After I told her that I finally found out who that officer was in my arms, she released me of any karmic oaths, obligations, vows and agreements. Later on that year, I moved out of her house feeling secure and ready to be without her in the world.

I am pretty sure that there is more than one karmic lesson in this life for me, and there were karmic lessons involved for my parents of that lifetime also. What is interesting is that most of my mother's children in this lifetime wore uniforms for either or both school and career at one time or another. And what about my fiancée from that lifetime? Well, we had been a couple in a previous life where she was a man and I was a woman, and later on, we reunited in the mid to late 1800's where I was once again a man, Captain Matthew Weber and she was Madelaine. That is another story to tell later.

***I know that this is a random place to start picking out lives to recant but it is the first one that I had "seen".

1800's Slave in the South

Time period: 1820's-1840s
Gender: male
Nationality: First generation African-American Slave
Married
Two children: boys
Three different slave plantations

"Jimmy Crack Corn and I don't care…", so I am skinny and lanky holding some kind of candle holder, walking through a cave like tunnel, singing this tune… though in this present life I had never heard of this tune. I am feeling free for the first time in my life! I see myself wearing a beige or off-white shirt and pants.

I was conceived on a slave plantation in Kentucky and then separated from my father. My mother, brother and I were taken from Kentucky to another plantation in Louisiana. It was small compared to the plantation back in Kentucky. I never saw my father again.

I see a line of roses in front of the main home on the plantation with the animal pen on the left. There are beautiful Magnolia trees by the master's house. Back at my second home, where I grew up, a tobacco plantation in Tennessee which has a bunch of Magnolia trees. I have a wife and children. For the most part we are treated decently and with the other slaves, we are a big family. My mother is on this plantation. I have a little brother at the plantation also. I was transferred from this plantation for being "rebellious" and belligerent. I spoke out against a whipping that was not deserved to another resident slave.

I see a line of roses in front of the main home on the plantation with the animal keep onto the left. There are beautiful Magnolia trees by the master's house. I can also remember the trees with their weeping branches, there are weeping willows throughout the plantation. The smell of the fresh air, the gnats and bugs picking at me and the stinging on my back. I do not like getting stung with a whip on my back, well, in reality, who does? I do not hesitate to create such anger towards anyone who touches my back.

My wife and I were married, not in the Christian sense, though it was a ceremony and we and everyone else honoured and respected the tie. I remember her being very angry at me for speaking up. It was hard because I knew that it would be considered insubordination yet it was the right thing to do, even though it put my family at risk. She was very angry with me because it left her very vulnerable to the bitterness and vengefulness of the masters, especially after I was sent away. Her tears, the letters that she had snuck to send me were deep, sad and filled with love for me.

I had received a "good 'ol ass whipping" and was relocated to another plantation, far from my family to a plantation in Missouri where I worked with pigs. I was in my early twenties. My fondest memories were in the evenings when we would sing and dance. The new plantation was much stricter and on top of that they were tough on me due to my history. Somehow, I found out about an escape route through Tennessee. I went through it once and I think that is where I am singing the Jimmy Crack Corn song. Later, after I escaped, I helped my wife and two boys to escape. The escape was almost a success. I got my wife and sons across the river to safety, it was me that was captured. I pleaded with yearning eyes to my wife to flee. I was just happy to know that my family was safe and I fulfilled my duty as a father and husband.

My wife was a domestic/cook slave and wore a light blue dress. She could make an awesome sundried tomato corn bread with a green bean salad. I can recall in this lifetime, even though I am a woman today, how it felt to penetrate her. It is interesting because in this present life, I am a woman who is very much heterosexual but I can go back into that time and feel the intensity, the excitement, the lust, and the love we have for each other. The way I would grab her breasts, ravish her neck, and caress her shoulders and her body, on top of her, just lifting her hips, penetrating her body, just a little by little, going all the way in and feeling when I orgasm how my testicles would just go up and, oh, it was almost like there was a buzzing sound, then a pulling up with a rush of heat and oh, wow, then the blood just rushes up even to the head (the head on top of the neck, hahaha), the tingling in the fingers that it is even scary to not orgasm, holding it too long…the way I would nibble on her toes, the way I would make her laugh, her white teeth that would contrast against her beautiful skin. She was dark, she was beautifully dark. She was a very hard worker.

And my children, my loving children…

I somewhat knew how to read. I don't know why, but I did, not eloquently, nor on a high academic level. I was able to, I have to go back further to find out why it seems that so did she, my wife, on a low level, like a third/fourth grade level. She would tell me words from the old country. She had a nickname for me and the children. The children would help out with the chicken coups, with the eggs and the hens there. She made being owned by someone else worth it, otherwise I would not have been able to continue to live that way.

Being able to be with her and the children, was as if that area was my area, even though it was on the land of the master.

I "see" the scene where my wife is very angry with me for having spoken up, even though I know it was the right thing to do. It left her vulnerable because they sent me away. I just couldn't keep quiet, when they whipped my buddy. Seeing the vengefulness, the hatred, the lack of compassion that we were human beings, just made me want to tear them down. They were beasts and uncivilized. They called us beasts but they were the real beasts, it showed in the way they walked. They are disgusting, their hair all grungy and dirty and their teeth rotting. They were actually proud of behaving like beasts. They thought that they were better, in reality they were like overly dressed cannibals. It was so hot and they thrived off wearing these ridiculous clothes and trying to convince my wife and other people that that was a better way of life, though it was truly disgusting. It was gross. They would drink this stuff that would just make them all angry and mad inside which made them behave that way. And, yet, they would look forward to drinking more of it, and we, the slaves, feared it. It was when we would all want to get away, hide, and escape.

*** This next part I am expressing it as I "see" myself talking in that lifetime. We enjoyed our music, our drumming, our chanting, but that white folk, just so not good, horrible, horrendous. Who were they lying to that that was all okay. Oh they will get their own, Almighty God will give it to them. They will regret ever, thinking that they were different. I pray that I never be white. Pray that we always appreciate cultures from all over. The fruit tastes so much better, then they put all this stuff, alcohol ruining the apples. It makes no sense; they make no sense. Just because they can speak in all these words and phrases… they are lying, it is all a smokescreen because their actions are beastly and horrendous, uncivilized. They are savages. The tear down, Nature, the woods, to claim stuff. It's not right. They are not good in the head. Never want to be them. I am happy that I am not. My mother suffered so much, the indignities. The white men are greedy, they are sick with greed, it penetrates them and then they create such lies, saying that they are in the right. Creating such circles, ridiculous fantasies, trying to capture and involve others, to get everybody else to believe, to want to give into their greed, their sickness that pollutes each one of them. It slowly pollutes us. I see my brother believing that their way of life is better, but it is not. Not that our way of life is better, it is not, but there is something else…I would hear stories of the old world from my mom, about the freedom, about the trees and being with nature, about the sand, the dirt and the rivers. But how, it all belonged to the animals, we were just caretakers of Mother Nature, not to disturb Mother Nature, but to be a part of it. Here is all this extra abundance for what, they do not know even what to do with it. They makeup artificial things saying how wonderful it is to use it, all this greed from what they get in return from the crops…they really do not need any of it. They are still savages, they are still beasts. They pet each other on the back for corrupting themselves, their minds, their hearts, their souls and their bodies. We are truly ourselves, the stronger ones. We are truly closer with God for we are meek and poor but understanding. We eat more of the natural food. They don't even say a prayer of thanks, they just gobble into the food. There is no connection. They seem as if there is no connection, as if everything is separated. That is why we harvest the crops, because no good white man can release the intense beautiful energies of these crops as they need to be harvested.

My wife is slowly believing that their way of life is better, that being white is better. I have to get her out, I have to get the kids out. I do want my children to be educated so that they can see how wrong the white man is, to use that education, to use the white man's words against them. That is my true dream for my children, to see my wife dance freely, and sing, and chant and praise the Lord as beautifully as she always does. That is my wish for them. I know that they will change the world.

I was hung, I died in my 20's in 1845.

In this lifetime, I fulfilled a karmic debt to my wife and children for they are the same family I had back in Caledonia in the early 80's CE when we revolted from the Romans and during the revolt, other Romans captured our families and killed them. I had always felt that if I hadn't gone to revolt, my wife and children would still be alive. So, in this lifetime, it meant a lot to me to save my wife and children, so that they may lead a fulfilled life purpose that they didn't get to live in the life in Caledonia. It didn't matter to me that I was to hang because freeing my family was my drive and I had fulfilled that. I had no regrets, I was content and feeling very satisfied with fulfilling my life purpose and completing my karmic debts. I was just happy to know that my wife and children were free and able to live a full life. I protected them and I freed them. Know that I love you all.

My present life's consolation is that as a man, I did know how to love a woman deeply and hopefully romantically, because there are other lives where I love a woman, but it doesn't seem that I know how to love a woman deeply, passionately.

Early 1900s Tango Dancer

Born: 1884
Gender: Male
Died: 1912, in France

I was a Jewish immigrant from Southeast Italy. I immigrated to Argentina, received by my uncle at the age of 12 years of age. We were jewelers in Argentina. I was fascinated with the Tango. It was danced on the street corners under the street lamps.

I was tall, wavy hair, coming from Italy because I had gotten into a fight with a son of an important man and had beaten up that kid. My parents, who feared any repercussions, sent me to Argentina to meet up with my mom's brother. He was a jeweler, catering to the rich in Argentina. I traveled on a huge ship, full of Italian immigrants such as myself. It was a long voyage, I hung out with the men, I learned to play cards, dance and read poetry.

In Argentina, I live with my uncle, and during the day I run errands for him, back and forth between buyers and other jewelers. In the evenings I watch the guys dance under the lamp post, some kind of competition they have.

There is an incident, it affects my whole short life. One night, after an evening of my uncle and his friend's drunken times, I am sleeping in another room, my uncle passed out, I feel something against my lips and I awaken. My uncle's friend is rubbing his sadden penis along my lips, he laughs, I am angry and back-handed him in his groin, I hate him. I start to hate every homosexual man, from now on.

I am going to stop here to interject some present day thoughts and apprehensions. When I first had a glimpse of this lifetime, I was all happy and proud because I love to dance. I, in this lifetime, even had taken tango lessons, aside from getting my Master's in Spanish with the theme…" The history of the Latinos through music and dance". "Seeing that I was a performer dancer, just made so much sense to me of how I have performed different dance styles throughout my present life. We tend to forget that each of us has our pains and are trying to complete our karmic debts and fulfill our lifetime's soul purpose, no matter how wonderful our talents and passions fulfill our ego.

There was a part of me when I saw the pain and anger of this lifetime, that was thinking of omitting the acknowledgement of this lifetime…but that would not be respectful to my soul who is ever connecting more and more with my spirit. By denying the tango dancer lifetime would be denying myself. So, I continue with what I "saw". In this present life time, I went through a change of homophobic to having really close friends that are gay. Yet back in the late 1890s being called gay were fighting words, hence why I kicked that kid's ass real good who had teased me and getting sent to Argentina. And now, the whole incident with my zio's amici didn't help my masculine self-confidence. In Argentina, during my teenage years I would doubt my sexuality, due to those two incidents and also to my surroundings.

After work, where it was mostly men, I would hang out at the street corner under the lamp posts with the other guys, gambling and competing in dance. There were hardly any women in our city. All us guys, if we won a few coins, would rush and show them to the few "mujeres" to see if they would give us sex, yes "give" us sex. None of us guys knew anything about romance or making love, so, due to my awesome dance competing style, I got sex often, hahaha, mostly to prove I was a man.

At the shop, my zio and I were dressed as if we had money. He would always say that, "people tend to spend money with other people who can appreciate good money" (meaning, if you look like that you have good taste, they will respect your tastes). So, even though we lived in a one-bedroom apartment, my zio, spent a lot of money on pretenses, we had about three fancy suits, a phonograph (one of the first people to have one in the jewelry district, which attracted people with money, including rich confused pansies), fancy kettles, cups and saucers (that were imported from Europe, with help from my parents, of course. They were cheap in Europe but because they were from there, people thought them expensive in Argentina.), and our "cultured" style, (we both spoke Italian, Hebrew and now, Spanish) and let us not forget my dashingly good looks as I grew into a handsome tall man, at least that is what the "mujeres" would tell me.

So, when I was about 17 years and approached by this pathetic rich pansy to go dance, I did. When I gave him sex, it was rage-revenge sex, saying, "I am not gay, I am just giving it you." He liked being shamed and humiliated while being dominated in gay sex, and he paid me well. He had a couple of other sad lost pansies that would request my attention and paid well they did.

After a couple of years saving from my services, I let that go and my zio and I were able to open another shop in Buenos Aires, where I started dancing in a group performing. No longer confused and "outgrew" my homosexual phobia rage, I enjoyed women more.

When I was about 25 years, I met a beautiful young socialite who was a bit rebellious and I married her. I still performed Tangos and other dances, and when I was about 26, my dance troupe went on tour. I couldn't afford to take my wife with me. I had danced and performed with well-known recorded milongo artists on tour in Panama, Mexico, east coast US, France, Belgium, Austria, Russia, Switzerland and as far away as Greece (there was a WW going on, also known as the European War to those from the Americas). I was able to sneak off into Italy and to visit my ma mama and siblings, for my papapa had already passed away some seven years before.

The visit was precious in my heart, I had always promised my family of my return and brought them beautiful gifts, reunited with my cousins and revisited the towns. Oh, how I missed linguini with mussels, pasta primavera with shrimp, flat bread and pesto with my risotto.

When it was time to meet up with my dance troupe in France, my sister and her little son went with me. We took in the sights of Paris and other cities. It seems that my face didn't go unnoticed, for one afternoon, while walking with my sister and her son, these three men in suits approached me and dragged me to the end of the alley, where they stabbed me in my gut and repeatedly kicked me and stomped on me....it was payback for a "gambling debt" (it was a brother of one of the pansies that I had serviced about seven years before.

I remember lying there, in a haze, head on the ground, wondering, "does 'she' love me?" I was now 27 years of age. I left behind my very old zio and wife, no children. As I am losing life, I remember thinking that ultimately, justice was done. My guilt for the rage-revenge sex I gave during those two years of 17-19 years of age, and how it caught up with me, it always does, and my ego saying, but oh I was handsome and a tremendous dancer. I wink and smile to myself as I float away.

Hawaii 1900s

Time period: 1920s-1960s
Gender: male
Status: married twice
Children: two
Died: 1966
Astrological Influences: Aquarius, Taurus, Libra, Gemini, Scorpio, Leo, Uranus in Pisces, Neptune in Leo, Pluto in Cancer, NN in Scorpio-Cancer

This is a very dear past life. Of course all the past lives are dear, and this past life in particular was my latest before this present one. This past life explains certain unexplainable feelings I had and still have regarding descending planes, the smell of gardenias, hula dancing, wearing flowers in my hair, surfing and just a deep love for Hawaii. In this present lifetime, I continued my love for Hawai'i by spending my Sweet 16 in Oahu with my friends who were doing their High School Senior Trip there, I also, did several active duty tours at NTCC Pearl Harbor in the Naval Reserve, and in Maui I had my honeymoon (from my first marriage). And just to emphasize my adoration of Hawai'i, I still dance, perform and coach Hawai'ian Hula (shout out to my Kumo Auntie Toni Stewart).

I used to have a fear of planes descending towards me, not that I was a target, but in my direction. The first time I encountered this light fear was when I was stationed on the Naval Air Station on Coronado Island in the Navy. I was going for a morning run on the base and low and behold an airplane was descending. Now I must include that the running course surrounded the landing strip, so this situation was quite normal, with enough clearance for the airplanes to land without hitting any runners. So I am running, in my own little world, I see this plane descending right in my path. Instead of running faster, I froze and slightly freaked out. I ducked deep, covering my head. I had such a shock. I finally shook it off and continued to run. The pilot and his buddy were laughing. I felt ridiculous, for of course the base was not going to put a runner's course in harm's way. Nevertheless, as I laughed with the pilots, there was this unsettled instinct of discomfort.

This takes me to my first scene of this past life. I "see" myself as a man, in my early twenties, with my mother, and another guy, we are looking up at the sky. We had just gotten out of church, or perhaps going into church. I had a yellow shirt on, wavy hair and a well-shaped physique, so did my brother, or at least I called him brah…he could have been a cousin or another guy. We saw all the Japanese planes flying towards us, it was scary because we were high up and we could almost see the pilots. It was also scary because as our eyes follow the planes, we see them attack the harbor down below and all the explosions. I remember thinking that it would take a good 45 minutes to an hour to get down there. I worked on base as a civilian, doing some sort of gardening and landscaping and perhaps some maintenance. I recall that my brah and I bid goodbye to my mom, who reluctantly sees us leave as we make the ride to Pearl Harbor.

So, a bit of background of who I am. I was born in the early 1920s. My name starts with a "K", I know, that sure narrows it down a lot, hahaha. I was actually born on Maui, then moved to Oahu. I was teaching at the elementary school while studying at the University of Hawaii on Oahu. I was studying Hawaiian botany. My Hawaiian language capabilities was okay, but not full on conversations, since my mother's time, the state government imposed restrictions on its usage. I enjoyed surfing, kayaking and walking through the natural Hawaiian gardens. I lived with my mother, brother and my father who had just passed away within the past two years of the bombing. My sister was married with children, she was older and I was a middle child.

I married after the war to a petite beautiful girl with dimples. She was my first wife. She was of Filipino and Japanese descent; her mother Filipino and her father Japanese. She was an airline stewardess. We had a daughter together. She died in 1949 in an airplane crash, the same year that the song "My Sweet Gardenia Lei" came out. That song forever represents my love for her. She was so dainty, petite and feminine, she made my heart sing. I did sing also and played the guitar, all the guys in my family played the guitar. When she died, I was devastated, I was left alone with my daughter. I moved in with my mother to help me care for my daughter. I gained a bit of weight, continued to study. My mother died a few years later.

Having lost my father, my wife and baby (she was pregnant when she died), and now my mother has become overwhelming for me, though I have my older sister still, I am starting to feel lost, without much roots. My daughter and I moved in with my sister, her husband and kids. I wanted my daughter to have a sense of unity and family, even though in my soul I was breaking apart more and more. No matter how hard I try to focus on what I have, I lament and yearn for the love and safety of the family I no longer have. I really try to immerse myself into my great surroundings, teaching, writing, being a father and hanging out with my sister and my cousins.

For a bit of a whole life seems to be getting better and more positive. The children, my students and my daughter keep me happy. I met a kind and supportive young lady. She is nice and cute. I decide to ask her to marry me, and she accepts. I am happy, not like I was before, at least happier than I have been for a while. My daughter now has someone, a female role model, besides my sister, that can guide her.

My sister and I had such a habit of eating huge breakfasts, after all breakfast was the most important meal of the day, right? (at least that was the perspective of society in those days of the Americans). We would eat pancakes with tons of butter, jam and maple syrup, with of course, slices of bacon, and a side of fruit. Who knew that that would be our downfall, our killer, and yet it gave us such a connection to our parents, where else do you think that we learned it from? We were all diabetic and with high cholesterol. Eating was our connection, and connecting made us happy.

My wife gave birth to my son. I feel so very lucky and happy to have someone to follow me around through the gardens of Hawaii and to take out into the ocean and see the sea turtles. My daughter is growing up beautifully and my wife is a great cook with a contagious laughter. Then the news hits me hard. My son is about 4 or 5 years of age, my daughter is 12 or 13 and I have been married for about 4 years now. I get a call from my sister's husband, she is dead. My last string of my life web has been cut (now, I was a middle child yet I do not recall well my younger sibling for whatever reason, hmm). I am lost, who do I have to unconditionally love me? Who will keep my family alive in my heart? I do not feel that I could do this alone. My beloved Hawaii is no longer. Again, I lose myself in despair, the pain and loss is so great that it doesn't allow me to see what I do have, my two lovely children and a good and kind wife. I am no longer a child, I no longer have the safety for the child within me. How can I lead my family when I do not even know where I am going. My sister was my North Star. I lose track of myself, I eat and drink all day, trying to keep some kind of emotional connection. I blew up to 175 pounds in a matter of six months. Because I continued to gain weight, I died of a heart attack within 6 years of my sister dying, at an agricultural conference in DC, where I was a speaker.

This lifetime was learning how to deal with family losses, being my own person, being my own roots to the universe, and I didn't do too well. I left behind a kind and beautiful wife, a darling daughter and son. My daughter doesn't even have blood relatives left, her step mother raises her. I know that as I write this story, I still have a child, a descendant still out there living, maybe not with my name, but with my blood. The irony is, I had feared not having real blood connections and I left behind my children. I can see how selfish my depression was and very irresponsible. And in this lifetime, I ask their forgiveness and my own and send much gratitude to my wife who raised the children that I couldn't. Much Mahalo!!!

In Retrospect

I still have so many questions about each one of my past lives, and probably always will. I have learned a lot about history, my karma, my soul purposes and soul connections.

So, now we are in present day California...no longer a past life, yet a life full of adventures, connecting, "seeing" and healing. My Soul, in past lives, has loved, hated, conceived, killed, explored, planted roots, spoken my mind, broken laws and boundaries, been a coward and chickened out, been famous, been reckless, danced, wrote books, kayaked, rode horses, prayed, healed, swam, escaped, enjoyed, given safe haven, been raped, hanged, cared for, persecuted, adored and most of all...LIVED!!!

Going through the astrological houses of a chart, I can relate how my soul's purposes and karmas have travelled, not necessarily in order, through the different houses to experience the multitude of life aspects. Every house and sign have different soul purposes. That means there are about 12x12 = *8.91610045E12* possibilities of soul purposes. WOW! That is a lot, yet each soul purpose is embedded into serving humanity in one way or another, and if we are lucky we do this through our passions and talents. Reviewing these lives, I fill very fulfilled in knowing that I have touched many souls, and hopefully for the majority of times, in positive ways.

There are still a few other lives that I have yet to include such as my life as a horse, an Italian monk, blue bubble life, green life, owning a winery around Montenegro, daughter of a giant, and slave/wife of an Egyptian tradesman (I think that it is in Egypt). I shall include these in my second book. I am waiting for clarity. Thank you for joining me on my journey. I do hope that this encourages you to take the time, relax and open yourself to "seeing".

Printed in the United States
by Baker & Taylor Publisher Services